Wonders of World Cultures

Exploring Asia and Oceania

Interdisciplinary Readings and Activities

written and illustrated by

Toni Rhodes

J. WESTON

WALCH
PUBLISHER

Portland, Maine

About the Author

Toni Rhodes has a master's degree in education from Georgia State University, Atlanta, Georgia. She was a teacher in the Atlanta area for ten years. Currently, she is focusing on educational writing, especially in the area of history, which has been a life-long interest. She writes a history-related children's column for a local newspaper and works in the Art History Department of Emory University, in Atlanta.

User's Guide
to
Walch Reproducible Books

As part of our general effort to provide educational materials which are as practical and economical as possible, we have designated this publication a "reproducible book." The designation means that purchase of the book includes purchase of the right to limited reproduction of all pages on which this symbol appears:

Here is the basic Walch policy: We grant to individual purchasers of this book the right to make sufficient copies of reproducible pages for use by all students of a single teacher. This permission is limited to a single teacher, and does not apply to entire schools or school systems, so institutions purchasing the book should pass the permission on to a single teacher. Copying of the book or its parts for resale is prohibited.

Any questions regarding this policy or requests to purchase further reproduction rights should be addressed to:

Permissions Editor
J. Weston Walch, Publisher
321 Valley Street • P. O. Box 658
Portland, Maine 04104-0658

1   2   3   4   5   6   7   8   9   10
ISBN 0-8251-3728-4

Contents

Introduction

This book focuses on the history and cultures of Asia and Oceania. The term *Oceania* refers to Australasia (Australia and New Zealand), Melanesia, Micronesia, and Polynesia.

Each chapter tells a story of a cultural treasure or "wonder" of Asia or Oceania. Section 1 focuses on the interpretation of archaeological artifacts, such as the contents of the frozen tombs found in southern Siberia. These artifacts are the clues that lead to theories about how ancient people lived and worked. Students are invited to play the role of archaeologist and think of theories based on the clues provided in the chapters.

Section 2 focuses on other cultural wonders of Asia and Oceania, presented in a straightforward, narrative format.

Activities in each chapter provide opportunities for students to learn more about the cultures that each wonder comes from. Many of the activities engage the students in experiential and interdisciplinary learning—instructional practices recommended by the National Council for the Social Studies in its report "Social Studies in the Middle School."

In the report, the NCSS recommends experiential learning because "all of us learn by doing. It follows, therefore, that middle level students benefit from concrete experiences such as role-playing, interviewing, community service, and similar activities in which they are able to analyze a common experience and explore ideas and values." The report states that interdisciplinary instruction focuses upon a central theme and draws from two or more subject areas. "The skills and knowledge gained from study involving a variety of disciplines enhances the social studies program as well as other parts of the curriculum."

It is hoped that you and your students will learn more about the wonders of our world's cultures through these readings and activities. Enjoy them!

Time Line of Dates

from Chapters in This Book

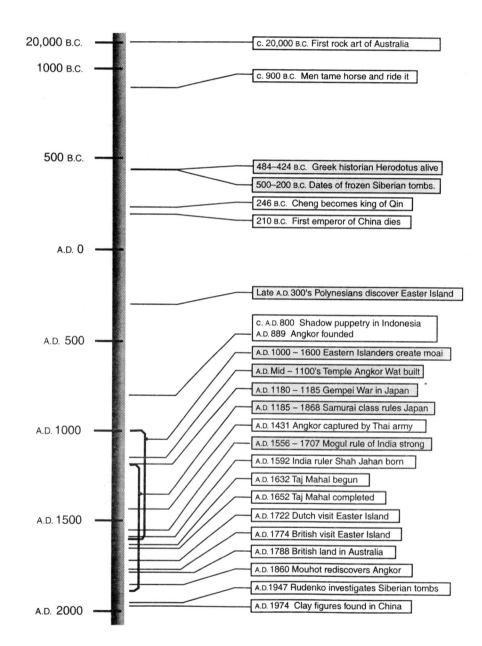

- 20,000 B.C. — c. 20,000 B.C. First rock art of Australia
- 1000 B.C. — c. 900 B.C. Men tame horse and ride it
- 500 B.C. — 484–424 B.C. Greek historian Herodotus alive
- 500–200 B.C. Dates of frozen Siberian tombs.
- 246 B.C. Cheng becomes king of Qin
- 210 B.C. First emperor of China dies
- A.D. 0
- Late A.D. 300's Polynesians discover Easter Island
- c. A.D. 800 Shadow puppetry in Indonesia
- A.D. 889 Angkor founded
- A.D. 500
- A.D. 1000 – 1600 Eastern Islanders create moai
- A.D. Mid – 1100's Temple Angkor Wat built
- A.D. 1180 – 1185 Gempei War in Japan
- A.D. 1185 – 1868 Samurai class rules Japan
- A.D. 1000 — A.D. 1431 Angkor captured by Thai army
- A.D. 1556 – 1707 Mogul rule of India strong
- A.D. 1592 India ruler Shah Jahan born
- A.D. 1632 Taj Mahal begun
- A.D. 1652 Taj Mahal completed
- A.D. 1500 — A.D. 1722 Dutch visit Easter Island
- A.D. 1774 British visit Easter Island
- A.D. 1788 British land in Australia
- A.D. 1860 Mouhot rediscovers Angkor
- A.D. 1947 Rudenko investigates Siberian tombs
- A.D. 2000 — A.D. 1974 Clay figures found in China

General Outline of This Book

I. Time Line

The time line shows the dates and events included in each chapter. You can copy the time line for students to refer to as they read.

II. Internet Sites

This page includes a list of Internet sites that are relevant to Asia and Oceania.

III. Introductory "Clues and Theories" Activity

Introduce your students to the field of archaeology by taking them through the activity on page *ix*. The goal is to help students see what objects from the past (**clues**) can tell about people and cultures in history (**theories**). Students will sharpen their skills in determining relevance of information and drawing conclusions. They will practice communicating their theories and backing them up with clues. This will provide some practice for Section 1, where they read and then draw their own conclusions about archaeological discoveries.

IV. Chapters

  A. Teacher Guide Pages

  • Provide a Chapter Summary, which defines the "wonder" and lists the major themes covered in the chapter.

  • Give answers to "Think About It," "Your Theory," and "Thought/Discussion Questions."

  • Include a bibliography, including adult and juvenile books and magazine articles.

  B. Reading about a "Treasure" or "Wonder" Centered in Asia or Oceania

  Section 1: Archaeological Wonders (artifacts)

  • "Think About It" questions in the reading help students reflect on the material.

  • "Your Theory" boxes let students play the role of archaeologist.

  Section 2: Cultural Wonders of Asia and Oceania (expands the concept)

  • "Think About It" questions in the story help students reflect on the material.

  C. Activities to Enhance Student Understanding

  • Many activities are "hands-on" and give students a chance to learn by doing.

  • If students do all activities, they will use skills and knowledge from at least two disciplines.

  Activities include: step-by-step instructions, objectives, time needed to complete the activity, suggested number of students, and materials.

  D. Thought/Discussion Questions to Enhance Student Understanding

  • These questions help students focus and expand on information in the chapter.

Internet Sites

Please keep in mind that Internet sites change constantly; therefore, the ones listed below may have moved or changed since this book was published. These sites were chosen based on their potential to be permanent Internet sites and their established credentials.

General Interest—Asia

Asia Society
www.askasia.org

Includes:
- Information/News of Asia
- Instructional resources, such as lesson plans, maps, bibliographies, reviews

Japan

National Museum of Japanese History
trisun.rekihaku.ac.jp/rekihaku/index.html

- Photos of artifacts in galleries

Australia

Southern Arrernte Aboriginal Tribal Group of Central Australia
aboriginalart.com.au/

Includes information about:
- Community, Arrernte, dreamtime, tourism, links, playing the didgeridoo, Aboriginal arts

Edward A. Clark Center for Australian Studies
http://www.utexas.edu/depts/cas/index.html

Includes:
- Photo of aboriginal bark painting

The Cleveland Museum of Natural History
http://www.cmnh.org/research/cultural/aboriginal/expressions.html

This site features an exhibition called *Art of the Australian Aborigines* and includes:
- Brief history of aboriginal art
- Explanation of The Dreamtime
- Materials and designs of artwork
- Art revival
- Aboriginal children and their art

Bali and Beyond (a Los Angeles-based performing arts company inspired by the cultures of Indonesia)
http://www.balibeyond.com/gamelan/index.html

Includes information (and many photos) about:
- Shadow Theater (both Javanese and Balinese)
- Javanese Gamelan
- Balinese Gamelan
- Music samples (requires audio software)

Name _____

Date _____

Clues and Theories

> ◆ *Objective:* To think about how archaeologists find objects and study them, which leads to theories about how people lived in the past
> ◆ *Time to Complete Activity:* About an hour
> ◆ *Materials Needed:* Paper and pencil

Directions: Read the following story.

You are walking in the woods one day. You find a dirt road. This road leads to an old house. The door is hanging open, windows are broken, and weeds and vines have grown up. It looks as if no one has lived in the house for a long time. You decide to look around, and you find a few things left by people who had been in the house.

In one of the closets you find a scrap of newspaper that has a date: July 11, 1947.

In what was the kitchen, you find a broken glass milk bottle.

In the middle of one of the rooms, you see some burned logs, matches, and an empty sardine can.

Out in the yard, you find a long length of chain hanging from a tree limb and a large oily stain on the ground beside the house. In the bushes is a rusted metal tricycle with one wheel missing.

To your surprise, you also find a grave behind the house. The grave is very small and has a wooden marker on it that says "Fluffy."

- Think about the **clues** you found in the house and yard. Put these clues together to form your own opinions or **theories** about people who had been in the house—how they lived and played; what they ate; whether they were young or old; etc.

- Jot down your ideas.

- Discuss and exchange ideas with the others in your group.

SECTION I

Archaeological Wonders of Asia and Oceania

(Clues and Theories)

CHAPTER 1: Wonders in the Tombs of Siberia

Chapter Summary

What are the "wonders" in this story?

- The contents of the frozen tombs of southern Siberia excavated by the Russian archaeologist S.I. Rudenko in the 1940's.

What are the major themes covered in the story and activities in this chapter?

- The peoples of the steppes of Eurasia were the first to tame and ride the horse, which led to

dramatic changes in the lives of these horsemen and all who came in contact with them.

- The tribesmen of the steppes were not only fierce warriors; they were also skilled craftsmen, animal keepers, and artists, who were very successful at living in the harsh environment of southern Siberia.

Answers to "Think About It" Question

(page 8)

The Persian Empire was centered in what is now Iran.

Answers to "Your Theory"

(pages 7, 8)

The Body of an Older Man

Rudenko thought that the older man could have been a high-ranking person in the tribe, possibly a chief, because of his tattoos, a sign of high rank according to reports by Herodotus.

Fighting Warriors

The clues that Rudenko and the team found show that the Altai Mountain tribesmen fought like the Black Sea Scythians. They used bows and arrows, battle-axes—the cuts on the man's head were probably caused by an enemy's battle-ax—and protected themselves with shields. They also took scalps from enemies and were themselves scalped.

Nomads or Seminomadic Herdsmen?

Rudenko believed that the tribesmen were seminomadic; that is, they lived in one area for most of the year. Their skill in building log burial chambers was probably a result of building log homes that were more or less permanent structures.

A seminomadic lifestyle is also indicated by the type of animals they kept. The high-quality horses, sheep, and cattle (some with tender young) would need extra protection and a more permanent home than a purely nomadic lifestyle could give them. They especially needed protection inside an enclosure during the winter months.

Rudenko saw another clue in some of the bottles that were found—neither the heavy clay bottles nor the fragile ones could have been easily carried if the tribesmen were completely nomadic.

Their concern with wild animals and hunting could indicate that at one time the tribes had been more nomadic.

Contact with Other Cultures

Obviously the Altai tribes either had direct contact with Persians and with Chinese people, or at least contact with traders who went to Persia or China.

Also, their culture was similar in many ways to the Scythian culture. For instance, warriors of both cultures scalped enemies during fighting and used shields made of sticks. This shows that they had contact with the Scythians of the Black Sea region and were perhaps related to them.

Answers to "Cultural Contacts of Southern Siberian Tribes" _____

(page 11)

Lines would be drawn from the site of the frozen tombs in southern Siberia to China and Persia because the story mentioned objects found in the tombs that had come from those two empires. This means that the tribesmen had contact with China and Persia, probably through traders. Another line would be drawn from the frozen tombs to Scythia. The story mentioned objects that showed Scythian contact, such as a design on a carpet showing a mounted warrior wearing his bow-and-arrow case in the style of the Scythians. Actually, the Scythians were probably distant relatives of the tribesmen of southern Siberia.

Answers to "Thought/Discussion Questions" _____

(page 12)

1. Answers could include the following:
   - People could travel a lot farther on horseback, so trading with other cultures increased.
   - As people on horseback gained a new sense of power and control over their environment, they began to imagine that the horse had mystical powers and even began to worship the horse.

2. Answers will vary.

3. Answers will vary.

Bibliography _____

Adult books

From the Land of the Scythians: Ancient Treasures from the Museums of the U.S.S.R., 3000 B.C.–100 B.C. New York: Metropolitan Museum of Art, 1975.

Frozen Tombs: The Culture and Art of the Ancient Tribes of Siberia. London: British Museum Publications Limited, 1978.

Rolle, Renate. *The World of the Scythians.* Berkeley: University of California Press, 1989.

Rudenko, Sergei I. (M.W. Thompson, trans.) *Frozen Tombs of Siberia.* Berkeley: University of California Press, 1970.

Trippett, Frank. *The Emergence of Man: The First Horsemen.* New York: Time-Life Books, 1974.

Magazine articles

Edwards, Mike. "Searching for the Scythians." *National Geographic,* Vol. 190, (Sept. 1996), pages 54–79.

CHAPTER 1:
Wonders in the Tombs of Siberia

Clothing, saddles and saddle covers, rugs, and many other objects found in frozen tombs in southern Siberia had cutout designs of animals.

ASIA

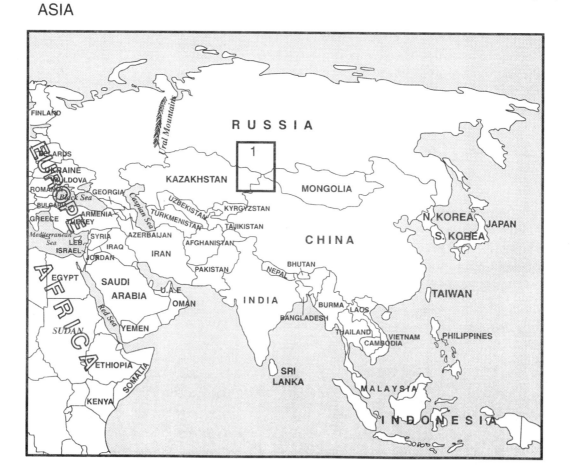

 The focus of this chapter is the tribes of southern Siberia from 500 to 400 B.C.

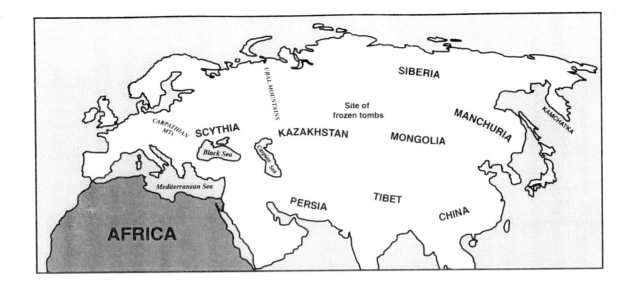

The First Horsemen

Historians believe that sometime around 900 B.C., farmers who lived on the vast, dry, grass-covered plains (called *steppes*) between the Carpathian Mountains and Mongolia tamed the horse and began to ride. This changed their lives dramatically. They became nomadic—that is, they moved from place to place on horseback, herding sheep and cattle, looking for grass for their animals to eat, and sometimes hunting wild animals.

They also became fierce warriors on horseback, especially using bows and arrows.

One of the richest and most powerful of the nomad tribes was the Scythians, who lived north of the Black Sea. The Scythians did not leave any written records, so what we know about them comes mainly from Herodotus, a Greek historian, and from objects found in their magnificent tombs.

Herodotus lived from about 484 to 420 B.C. He visited Greek trading ports on the Black Sea and wrote about the Scythian tribes who lived in the region. Some of what he wrote was probably legend rather than things that he actually saw, but archaeo-logical finds have shown that some things that he reported were true.

Herodotus described the Scythians as fierce warriors. He wrote that they cut off the heads of enemies killed in battle, then emptied the skulls to use as drinking cups. A fighter on horseback would scalp dead enemies and hang the scalps from his horse's bridle. The more scalps a warrior collected, the more he was respected. When two warriors promised something to each other, they cut themselves, mixed their blood together, then drank the blood.

A fourth century B.C. gold plaque found in a tomb shows two Scythian men pledging their friendship to each other by drinking from a cup filled with wine and drops of their own blood. This would seem to back up what Herodotus said about the way warriors made promises to each other.

Herodotus also wrote about the Scythians' great wealth, which came from taxing everything that passed through their land on the way to the Greek trading cities on the Black Sea.

The Scythians had complicated and long-lasting burial traditions, according to Herodotus. When a king died, their mourning period lasted for forty days. Some of the men cut their hair, ears, foreheads, noses, and arms and stuck arrows in their left hands. After the king's body was stuffed with herbs and seeds for preservation, it was carried to the grave, followed by a long line of grieving tribesmen. When the body was laid in the grave, many of the king's servants were strangled and placed in the grave along with sacrificed horses.

Grave Goods Tell a Story

Nomad-made objects. We also know something about the Scythians and other nomadic tribes from objects that grave robbers left behind in the burial mounds.

Metal ornaments found in the graves were worn on clothing and horse equipment. They show how important various animals were in the lives of the people.

Male reindeer, elk, and red deer, called stags, are portrayed quite often. Their antlers are usually huge.

Big cats are often shown with exaggerated teeth and muscles. According to some scholars, nomad warriors may have worn plaques with cat images in the hope of taking on the big cat's fearsome qualities.

Birds of prey, such as hawks, appear bigger than in life and able to bring down game much larger than themselves. This could show the spiritual importance of birds of prey to the tribesmen.

A common theme in the ornaments is the life-and-death struggle between the weak and the strong. Sometimes the strong predator is an imaginary beast.

Greek-made burial objects. Scythians were wealthy enough to hire Greek artisans to make gold and silver bowls, sword scabbards (holders), and jewelry. These items provide a visual record of Scythian dress and activities.

One of the most spectacular finds from a Scythian grave is a gold breastplate, weighing two and a half pounds. It consists of three bands containing many figures that show details of Scythian life. In the center of the top band, two bearded shirtless men appear to be stretching a woolly sheep's pelt. Each man keeps his bow-and-arrow case nearby, in case of danger. The other figures on the band are going about their business—a foal is nursing its mother; a shorn sheep is being milked by a squatting man.

In his History in Nine Books, Herodotus describes how a Scythian warrior scalped his slain enemies: "He makes a groove around the head near the ears; then he holds the head in his hands and pulls off the skin; then he scrapes off the fat with an ox rib and works it in his hands to make it soft; now he can use it as a duster and hangs it from the bridle of the horse he rides; he is then very proud of himself."

Follow Along with Professor Rudenko

These findings and the reports by Herodotus provided priceless information about the Scythians, but a Russian archaeologist named S. I. Rudenko wanted to find out more. While exploring a cold, mountainous region in southern Siberia, Rudenko discovered something truly unusual—frozen tombs in which were preserved many objects that usually decay and disappear over time (see map previous page). He found a collection of everyday things—a woman's pigtail, a man's false beard, rugs, cushions, saddles, wooden tent poles—that brought the culture of the tribesmen to life.

Follow along as Professor Rudenko and his team explore the frozen tombs of horsemen who were much like the Scythians. You will get a chance to take on the archaeologist's role and form theories based on the clues that are found.

It is 1947, just after World War II. You have traveled to a high valley in a mountainous land. You find a fairly level area that is open and grassy. There are a few stands of larch trees. You immediately notice the huge mounds of stones that cover up five graves that Rudenko and his team have come to investigate.

Native workers help remove the rocks, some weighing several tons, from the central part of the mounds. Removing the rocks exposes the large support beams of the burial chamber. The beams have bowed under the weight of the rocks. The rest of the chamber is like a log cabin, with roof made of logs and walls made of planks.

The inside of the burial chamber is a solid block of ice. As the team carefully chips away the ice, objects that have been frozen for 2,400 years begin to emerge. Some of the coffins, made of huge hollowed-out logs, contain skeletons of the dead. Some coffins, much to Rudenko's delight, contain not just bones, but partially-preserved bodies of both men and women. Their prized possessions are scattered around and are in amazingly good condition. Workers spread out a beautiful rug, about 10 by 16 feet, and sew it to a lining to keep it from stretching.

After all the items have been carefully cleaned and studied, they provide clues that Rudenko uses to form theories about the people who lived here.

The Body of an Older Man

Clues. In Grave 2 you find a man's preserved body. According to Rudenko, he was about sixty years old, because his teeth are very worn.

His body is covered with tattoos. One of the tattoos looks like a griffin (head and wings of an eagle, body of a lion) with a long twisting tail that ends in a snake's head.

Rudenko recalls that ancient writers, including Herodotus, wrote that some tribes they met showed high rank or nobility by wearing tattoos.

> **✍ Your Theory**
>
> What ideas do you have about this older man whose body was found in a grave?

Fighting Warriors

Clues. Scattered in the graves are arrowheads made of antler bone and broken arrow shafts. A large carpet has a design showing a warrior on horseback wearing his bow-and-arrow case on the left, in the style of the Scythians.

The preserved head of an older male has deep cuts on the forehead that probably were the cause of death.

Another preserved head looks as if it was scalped.

You find shields made of round sticks lashed together with leather woven in patterns. Rudenko recalls that a gold comb from a Scythian tomb showed a similar type of shield.

> **✍ Your Theory**
>
> Can you help Rudenko think of some theories about how the tribesmen fought?

Nomads or Seminomadic Herdsmen?

Clues. Wood planks in the burial chambers are of uniform size and fit together very tightly, showing that the mountain tribesmen were very skilled at building wooden structures.

The tombs also contain preserved bodies of horses. Rudenko sees that some horses have a ring pattern in their hooves that shows that they lived through periods of famine. But, some of the horses are taller, without the ring pattern, as if they had been treated in a special way and did not have to go hungry.

You find the bones and partially preserved bodies of other animals, including sheep with fine-quality wool and cattle. Rudenko remarks that these animals would have to be protected in an enclosure during the bitterly cold winter in order to survive.

Heavy clay bottles and very thin-walled, fragile bottles are found in the graves. These would have been difficult to carry around.

Rudenko sees a clue that contradicts the other clues—many wild animals appear in the art of the tribesmen. Designs on their clothing and saddle covers show predators, like big cats, attacking hoofed animals, like deer. This shows an interest in hunting, which is one way that nomadic people get their food.

> ### ✍ Your Theory
>
> What do these clues tell you about the lifestyle of the tribesmen—were they nomadic, that is, traveling most of the time, or were they semi-nomadic, staying in one area most of the time?

Contact with Other Cultures

Clues. Rudenko wonders if the tribesmen traded with other cultures. He finds a clue in a cloth from Grave 5. A design in the cloth shows women standing around a censer, a container used to burn incense. Their right hands are raised in an attitude of prayer or respect. Rudenko recalls that designs on Persian-made objects show women in a similar position, holding up their right hands and standing around a censer.

A large cut-pile carpet found in one of the graves has an image of a horseback rider. The horse's tail is tied in a knot, and it wears a large feather on its head. This brings to mind Persian carpets, in which you have seen similar designs, including the knot and the feather, and you also recall that cut-pile carpets were made in Persia for centuries (and still are).

Chinese silks and a Chinese mirror are found in some of the graves. The team finds a cloth covering

used under a horseman's saddle. The silk cloth is covered with phoenixes and plant designs exquisitely embroidered in silk. Rudenko remembers that this kind of cloth was made in China for very rich people, especially as a marriage gift for a princess.

> ### ✍ Your Theory
>
> These clues obviously point to contact with what two Asian cultures?

The digging season is over here in the high valley. The harsh, bitterly cold Siberian winter will be closing in soon. You think about the tribesmen 2,400 years ago getting ready to settle into their log cabins for the winter, their animals protected nearby in an enclosure. Your discoveries in the graves have helped you form a picture of what life was like for them.

> ### Think About It—
>
> What modern country or countries are now in the area that once was ancient Persia?

Scenes of predators, such as birds or large cats, pouncing on other animals were common on many of the objects found in the graves.

Source: Travels in the Regions of the Upper and Lower Amoor and the Russian Acquisitions on the Confines of India and China, by Thomas Witlam Atkinson. (New York: Harper & Brothers, 1860.)

Name _____

Date _____

Leather Cutout Patterns

In the 1940's a Russian archaeologist named S. I. Rudenko dug up some frozen graves in southern Siberia that date from 500–400 B.C. Things that usually decay and disappear, like leather, wool, wood, cloth, and the bodies of horses and people, had been preserved in ice for 2400 years. Rudenko was able to form detailed theories about how these ancient Siberian tribes lived by studying the objects in their graves.

The skilled craftspeople in the tribe created beautiful cutout designs that they pasted or sewed on saddle covers, saddles, clothing, horse bridles, wall hangings, and many other things. Simplified designs of animals appear often in the cutouts. The most popular type of scene shows a predator, like a mountain lion, attacking a weaker animal, like a deer or a goat. Sometimes the predator would be a mythical creature—for example, a griffin.

◆ *Objective:* To make a cutout in the ancient Siberian style

◆ *Time to Complete Activity:* 1 hour

◆ *Materials Needed:* Unlined white paper, craft knife, small sharp scissors, black paper, piece of mat board or cardboard at least $8\frac{1}{2}$ by 11 inches, copy machine

---

Directions:

_____ Photocopy the design on this page onto a sheet of white paper, enlarging it if you like.

_____ Tape the copy of the design to the mat board, taping only the corners.

_____ Starting with the inside, use the craft knife to cut out the designs.

_____ After the inside designs are cut out, remove the paper from the mat board and cut out the whole picture with the scissors.

_____ Glue the cutout onto the black paper and frame if you like.

Variation: *Create your own cutout picture by first drawing a silhouette of an animal or flower, then designing the inside cut designs.*

Costume of a Southern Siberian Woman

In the 1940's a Russian archaeologist named S. I. Rudenko dug up some frozen graves in southern Siberia that date from the 500–400 B.C. Things that usually decay and disappear, like leather, wool, wood, cloth, and the bodies of horses and people, had been preserved in ice for 2400 years. Rudenko was able to form detailed theories about how these ancient Siberian tribes lived by studying the objects in their graves.

The people were very skilled at making and decorating clothing. To make cloth, they wove fiber from the hemp plant and also pressed wool to make a cloth called felt. They sewed with fine woolen thread.

They also made clothing from fur, which was stitched with sinew thread. (Sinew comes from tough animal tissue that connects muscle to bone.) Very often the furry side of the pelt was turned inward.

- ◆ *Objective:* To draw a picture of a Siberian woman's costume from reading a description
- ◆ *Time to Complete Activity:* 1 hour
- ◆ *Materials Needed:* Paper, colored pencils, dictionary, encyclopedia, other research materials

Directions:

_____ Read the following description of a woman's costume that Rudenko found in one of the frozen graves of southern Siberia.

_____ Draw a picture of the costume based on the description and also based on your research into the meaning of words like *caftan.*

In one of the graves a short caftan, with long narrow sleeves is found.

The caftan is made of squirrel skin with the fur turned inward. Fur extends beyond the end of the sleeves in the wrist area. To give the garment more body, lines of sinew stitching extend along the length of the sleeves and the front and back of the caftan. Bands of red leather cutout patterns decorate the sleeves and body of the caftan. On the outside of each sleeve, a 4-inch wide band extends from the top edge to the wrist area. On the body of the caftan, 3- to 4-inch wide bands extend from the neck area to the bottom edge. The designs in the cutouts look like rams' heads, roosters' combs, and lotus blossoms (see drawing).

Along the bottom of the caftan is a wide border of black colt's fur turned to the outside.

Another part of the woman's costume, a long apron made of pieces of squirrel and sable fur turned toward the inside, was found. It is rounded at the top and long enough to cover the front of a skirt. The bottom of the apron is not straight but curves up in the center. Like the caftan, it has lines of stitching extending from the top to the bottom.

It is decorated with three long, wide panels of leather cutout decorations on the front, extending from top to bottom. The outside edge is covered with fur dyed blue. Rams' heads and lotus flowers repeat in the design.

From parts found in the grave it was possible to put back together a woman's boot. The bottom of the boot looks like the shape of the foot and is covered with designs, mainly lotus flowers. It was sewn onto a top part that has a seam in back and attaches with pleats to the front, like a ballet slipper. Above that, there is a section of leopard fur turned outward, which would extend almost to the knee. The upper band of the boot is decorated with sinew in a looping pattern, and the edge is covered with red woolen braid.

Ram's head and lotus repeating pattern.

(At this time, historians are not sure what women wore underneath their aprons. No remains of women's skirts or trousers have been found in the frozen graves of southern Siberia, and women are not usually shown on artifacts found in Scythian graves.)

Cultural Contacts of Southern Siberian Tribes

In the 1940's a Russian archaeologist named S. I. Rudenko dug up some frozen graves in southern Siberia that date from 500–400 B.C. Things that usually decay and disappear—like leather, wool, wood, cloth, and the bodies of horses and people—had been preserved in ice for 2,400 years. Rudenko was able to form detailed theories about how these ancient Siberians lived by studying the objects in their graves.

Many of the objects show that the Siberian tribes traded with people of other cultures. For instance, seeds of the coriander plant were found. These seeds were used in ancient times as a medicine and for their pleasant odor. This plant does not grow naturally in southern Siberia, so it must have arrived there through trade with people from other parts of Asia.

> ◆ *Objective:* To locate other cultures who were in contact with the southern Siberian tribes
>
> ◆ *Time to Complete Activity:* 1 hour
>
> ◆ *Materials Needed:* Student pages for "Wonders in the Tombs of Siberia," map on this page; pencil; copy machine

Directions:

_____ If desired, enlarge the map on this page on a copier.

_____ Read the chapter, paying close attention to contacts the Siberian tribes had with other cultures, and draw lines from them to the site of the frozen tombs in southern Siberia.

> **Variation:** *Research the history of the plant called coriander. Where could it have come from? If you discover some possible locations, put them on the map.*

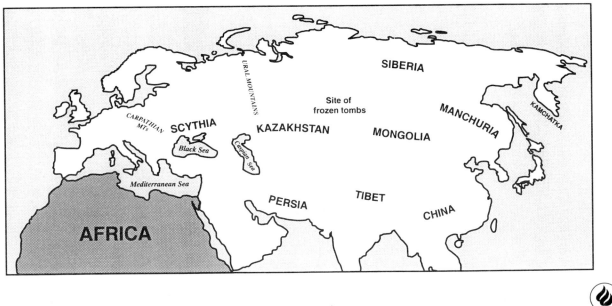

Name _____

Date _____

Thought/Discussion Questions

1. When the tribes of the steppes of Eurasia tamed the horse and began to ride, they became more nomadic and began to fight on horseback. What other changes do you think the horse brought into their lives?

_____

_____

_____

_____

2. Based on this reading, what do you think life would have been like for a young man or a young woman in the tribe?

_____

_____

_____

_____

3. Do any of the activities or objects of the Scythians or mountain tribes remind you of any other tribes that you have studied?

_____

_____

_____

_____

CHAPTER 2: The Giants of Easter Island

Chapter Summary

What are the "wonders" in this story?

- The huge statues of Easter Island are treasures of prehistoric Polynesian art and archaeology.

What are the major themes covered in the story and activities in this chapter?

- The Easter Islanders developed a robust prehistoric culture in which large numbers of people worked at creating, moving, and erecting large statues that represented ancestors of various clans on the island.

- Sometime in the late 1700's, the Easter Island culture collapsed, probably because of overpopulation and destruction of the island's forests, which led to famine and the toppling of the ancestor statues.

Answer to "Think About It" Question

(page 19)

Chile

Answers to "Your Theory"

(page 19)

Clues About Statue Carving

After looking at the clues, archaeologists have decided that the Easter Island craftspeople, who lived in nearby houses, used the palm-sized, basalt tools to carve the statues out from the tuff inside the volcanic crater, Rano Raraku.

Clues About How the Huge Statues Were Moved to Their Platforms

Archaeologists believe that after the statues were cut away from the rock bed of the crater, they could have been slid down the outside surface of the crater, then moved onto tree trunks used as rollers.

Another way statues could have been moved was on sledges (or sleds) made of tree trunks. The statues would have been tied onto the sledges with rope made of tree bark, or other native material. Then they would be dragged along a roadway by many people.

Clues About How the Statues Were Stood Up on the Platforms

Once the statue was rolled or dragged next to the base of the platform, it was probably raised gradually by using ropes to hold it securely and levers to move it little by little so stones could be slipped underneath (a ramp). Eventually, when there were enough stones under the statue and it was almost standing upright, it could be tipped over onto the platform.

Clues About the Islanders' Reasons for Making the Statues and Putting Them on Platforms

When the original Easter Islanders came from somewhere in Polynesia, they brought their ancestor worship with them. Archaeologists generally agree that the moai represent respected ancestors. After the statues were in place on their platforms, the white eyes would be placed into the eye sockets to bring the statue ancestors to "life."

Clans on the island competed with each other to build statues of their ancestors. Tattoos and loincloths that showed high rank were carved into the statues.

Clues About Why the Easter Islanders Knocked Down Their Statues

Archaeologists believe that an overpopulation of Polynesian rats ate the nuts of palms on the island, contributing to a severe decline in the number of trees. Fewer trees meant that the islanders could no longer build large enough canoes to go out into the rough seas for fish, a large part of their diet. (Trees, of course, were also cut down for cooking, building houses and boats, and possibly for transporting statues.)

The rats caused a decline in another staple of the islanders' diet—seabirds and their eggs. The eggs of the birds were eaten by the rats, so the birds could not reproduce.

Apparently, a severe shortage of food, especially protein, caused the islanders to start fighting with one another in competition for food. During the fighting, clans pushed down statues of competing clans.

Answers to "Thought/Discussion Questions"

(page 23)
1. Answers will vary.
2. Islanders cut down trees to clear land for growing food. Trees were also cut down to build canoes and houses, and to make rollers and ropes for moving and raising statues. Trees would also have been used for firewood.
3. Answers will vary.

Bibliography

Adult books

Bahn, Paul, and John Flenley. *Easter Island, Earth Island.* London: Thames and Hudson, 1992.

Heyerdahl, Thor. *Easter Island: The Mystery Solved.* New York: Random House, 1989.

Van Tilburg, Jo Anne. *Easter Island: Archaeology, Ecology, and Culture.* Washington, DC: Smithsonian, 1994.

Juvenile books

Mann, Peggy. *Easter Island: Land of Mysteries.* New York: Holt, Rinehart & Winston, 1976.

Meyer, Miriam W. *The Blind Guards of Easter Island* (Great Unsolved Mysteries Series). Chatham, New Jersey: Raintree/Steck-Vaughn Pub., 1983.

Magazine articles

Bahn, Paul G. "Making Sense of Rongorongo," *Nature,* Vol. 379 (January 18, 1996), pp. 204–205.

Brownell, M. Barbara. "Secrets of Easter Island," *National Geographic World,* n. 233 (January 1995), pp. 6–10.

Conniff, Richard. "Easter Island Unveiled," *National Geographic,* Vol. 183 (March 1993), pp. 54–79.

Wassmann, Cliff. "The Other Side of Easter Island," *Earth,* Vol. 4 (December 1995), pp. 78–79.

CHAPTER 2:
The Giants of Easter Island

The mysterious statues of Easter Island have baffled people since they were discovered by Europeans in the 1700's. This one is about 8.25 feet tall and weighs four tons.

OCEANIA

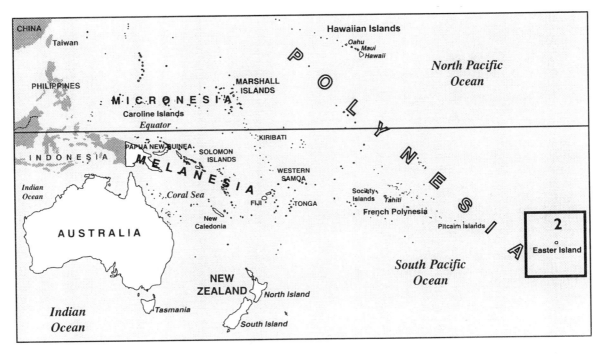

CHINA
Taiwan
PHILIPPINES
MICRONESIA
Caroline Islands
Equator
INDONESIA
PAPUA NEW GUINEA
SOLOMON ISLANDS
MELANESIA
Indian Ocean
Coral Sea
AUSTRALIA
New Caledonia
Tasmania
NEW ZEALAND
North Island
South Island
Indian Ocean

Hawaiian Islands
Oahu
Maui
Hawaii
North Pacific Ocean
POLYNESIA
MARSHALL ISLANDS
KIRIBATI
WESTERN SAMOA
FIJI
TONGA
Society Islands
Tahiti
French Polynesia
Pitcaim islands
2
Easter Island
South Pacific Ocean

② This chapter focuses on the Easter Island culture from the late 300's to the 1800's.

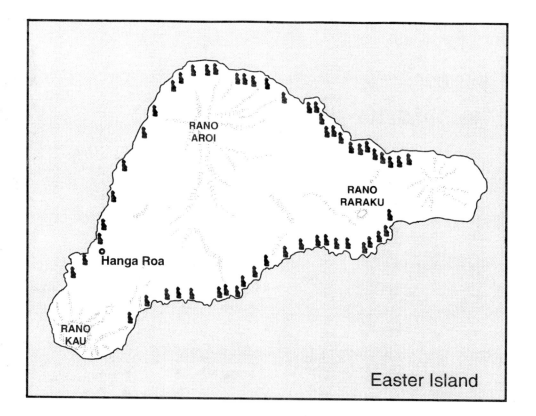

Easter Island

A Land unto Itself

Easter Island is the most isolated island with people living on it. It stands alone in the South Pacific Ocean on the edge of Polynesia, more than 1,400 miles from the nearest land.

Huge waves pound the coast of Easter Island, making it very difficult for boats to dock. Strong winds rake the almost treeless landscape, which is dotted with volcanic craters.

Only about 2,000 people live on Easter Island now, but once there may have been as many as 10,000 people living on this speck of land, which the natives call Rapa Nui.

The Mysterious Moai

Isolated Easter Island seems a very unlikely place to find huge stone statues of human figures. Determined islanders, however, did accomplish the task of carving between 800 and 1000 statues, which they call *moai,* during the period from A.D. 1000 to 1600.

Visitors to the island have raised some of the statues, which had been pushed down. The moai have long noses, jutting jaws, and were originally fitted with white staring eyes. They range in height from 6 to 33 feet, and one of the taller statues weighs 82 tons! The natives originally placed many of them on stone platforms. These platforms form an almost continuous wall along the coast of Easter Island (see map above).

Treasures of a Polynesian Culture

The huge statues and platforms are treasures of a unique and mysterious Polynesian culture that flourished on Easter Island. Archaeologists look for clues on the island to try to answer the following questions. How were the statues carved? How were they moved? How were they placed on the platforms? Why did the islanders undertake these massive carving and building projects? Why did the islanders topple their statues in the late 1700's?

On the next three pages you will explore Easter Island and find clues to answer these questions. You can take on the archaeologist's role and form theories about life on Easter Island based on the clues you find.

The giant statues of Easter Island, called moai by the islanders, are treasures of art as well as treasures of archaeology. Some have elaborate decorations on their backs. This statue is unusual because it was made of basalt rather than tuff, the volcanic stone used most often by the islanders. Illustration this page and page 19 from The Voyage of Captain Don Felipe Gonzalez in the Ship of the Line San Lorenzo, with the Frigate Santa Rosalia in Company, to Easter Island in 1770–1, Transcribed Translated, and Edited by Bolton Glanvill Corney (Cambridge: 1908.)

This statue is now in the British Museum.

Clues About Statue Carving

After a six-hour flight from Chile, you see Easter Island, a speck of land below in the vast blue Pacific Ocean. From the air you can make out several volcanic craters on the island.

After landing, you visit the volcanic crater called Rano Raraku. It is full of statues made of *tuff*, ash spewed out by the volcano thousands of years ago that hardened over time into rock. Some of the statues are finished and standing upright. Some are unfinished and lying on the slopes of the crater, as if they were asleep in their rock beds.

A few of the statues are almost completed and are only connected to the crater surface underneath by thin wedges of rock (see drawing on page 19).

Inside the crater, you find thousands of smallish pieces of basalt, a very hard volcanic rock. These appear to have been hit with other stones to flake pieces off, and they look like pointed tools. Many are just the right size to fit in the palm of your hand.

You remember that archaeologists digging inside and just outside the crater found the foundations of many houses.

Clues About How the Huge Statues Were Moved to Their Platforms

In your reading and in talking to present-day islanders, you learn that according to legend, the giant statues pulled themselves up out of their rock beds and walked slowly out of the crater, moving a little each day until they reached their platforms.

You find that more concrete evidence of how the statues got to their platforms is very rare on the island.

One clue other archaeologists have discovered is a Dutch drawing made in 1728, after Europeans discovered the island. The drawing shows a large sculpture (but not a moai) being moved on what may be rollers made of tree trunks, which were once plentiful.

You remember that when you were flying over the island, you saw faint traces of roadways leading away from the Rano Raraku crater. The roads looked like they had once been smoothed out and cleared of stones.

Other researchers in the 1950's interviewed older Easter Islanders. From information they provided, researchers made a sledge out of a tree trunk and tied a ten-ton statue to it with rope made of tree bark. About 180 men, women, and children were then able to pull the statue a short distance using ropes.

Clues About How the Statues Were Stood Upright on the Platforms

Again, you find few concrete traces of how the statues were moved to the base of the platforms, then raised in place. However, you do find the remains of a large ramp made of stones and rubble alongside one platform, and many other platforms have large piles of stones nearby that you think could be the remains of ramps.

Another thought comes to mind—the many trees that once covered the island also could have been used somehow to move the statues onto their platforms.

When Europeans discovered Easter Island, they all commented on its barren, treeless landscape. Clues to how the trees disappeared are found in remains of palm nuts with rat bites and many skeletons of the small Polynesian rat in archaeological digs.

Clues About the Islanders' Reasons for Making the Statues and Putting Them on Platforms

Like many other historians, you believe that late in the fourth century the Easter Islanders came from Polynesia, sailing vast distances across the Pacific Ocean. They probably came upon Easter Island by accident.

Their Polynesian origins contain clues about why the islanders made the giant statues.

From your studies you know that in general, most Polynesian cultures treated their great chiefs, warriors, and priests with respect and worshiped them after death (ancestor worship). Polynesians in the Marquesas Islands carved large stone statues and plat-

forms to keep alive memories of their great ancestors. Wooden statues with large staring eyes have also been found there.

After observing the Easter Island statues carefully, you realize that each giant statue is slightly different from the others, as if they were carved to represent individual people. Archaeologists have reported burial pits inside the sloping bases that lead up to the platforms.

After finding bits of broken eye pieces near the statues, researchers discovered that the figures placed on platforms had eye sockets, which once held white eyes with red pupils. The eyes, however, had fallen out or been plucked out by the natives. After some of the eyes were replaced in modern times, the statues appeared to be staring slightly toward the sky.

The first Europeans to visit Easter Island reported that while the islanders showed much respect for their statues, they did not call them gods. One statue was called a chief and other statues had nicknames like "Twisted Neck" and "Tattooed One."

Another clue you have found in your studies is the common Polynesian trait of competition among clans (family groups). For instance, tattooing that shows clan membership and rank among members was common throughout Polynesia. On Easter Island you see tattoo designs carved into the moai.

These marks made by islanders on a Spanish "treaty" of 1770 echo the rock art found all over the island. Some of the marks on rocks may have represented clan areas.

You also see the fold lines of a *maro* carved into the front and back of the statues. The maro was a special loincloth (a strip of cloth wrapped around the waist and between the legs) worn by Polynesians of high rank.

You know that scientists have dug up human skeletons on Easter Island that show common traits, as if there were several social groups that kept to themselves and did not marry into other groups. For instance, skeletons from one group were missing one corner of their kneecaps.

Rapa Nui stories, told to you and others through the years, tell of a group of royal islanders descended from the first ancestor, Hotu Matua. This group became the island's leading clan.

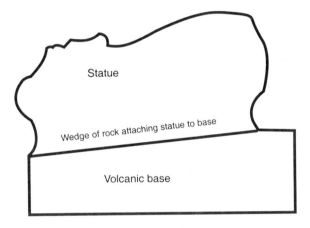

Statue

Wedge of rock attaching statue to base

Volcanic base

A few of the statues in the crater are unfinished and only connected to the crater rock underneath by thin wedges of rock. Also, bits and pieces of broken statues can be found throughout the crater.

Think About It—

Some people think that the original Easter Islanders did not come from Polynesia, but instead came from an area in South America. Which modern South American country do you think is in that area and now controls Easter Island?

Clues About Why the Easter Islanders Knocked Down Their Statues

Back home, you continue your research. You read that in 1774, a British ship that landed on the island reported seeing many overturned statues. What happened to cause the islanders to destroy their monuments, you wonder?

You find one clue to this mystery in reports by the first visitors. Europeans who visited in the early 1700's reported that the islanders did not have weapons but that some had cuts on their bodies. The British visitors of 1774 reported that the natives had clubs and spears made of sticks, with points of black lava.

Why would the islanders begin to fight with one another? You have seen clues to answer this question in the wooden statues made on the island that show men with hollow cheeks and bony rib cages. Visitors also reported seeing skinny, miserable islanders and said that it was difficult to find enough seabirds, fish, and chickens to eat.

The Dutch visitors in 1722 said that the islanders came out to meet them in leaky canoes made of small pieces of wood. However, rock art picturing large canoes and canoe ramps around the island shows that at one time the islanders had better boats.

You see other clues to the islanders' condition in archaeologists' reports that most of the remains of palm nuts had tooth marks of the Polynesian rat. You recall that even in modern times these rats can be a nuisance, eating birds' eggs and the nuts of plants.

Your Theory

From your observations on the island and from talking to islanders, after reading the reports of archaeologists and the first European visitors to the island, you have found clues to explain how and why the islanders made their giant statues and why they came to tear them down. What are your theories about life on Easter Island?

The Birdman Cult

The Easter Islanders came from somewhere in Polynesia and landed on Easter Island at the end of the fourth century. They developed a culture based on farming, fishing, capturing seabirds and their eggs, and eating the animals they brought with them, including the chicken and the small Polynesian rat, a staple of their diet.

The islanders also developed a complex system of ancestor worship, for which they created hundreds of huge statues. The clans (family groups) competed to create the best and biggest ancestor statues.

Sometime in the late 1700's, the Easter Island culture broke down because of overpopulation and extreme competition for food. The islanders fought with one another and knocked down the ancestor statues of rival clans. Two main clans emerged, headed by warrior chiefs.

Instead of practicing ancestor worship, the islanders began to worship the creator god Makemake. The Birdman Cult developed to decide which clan would rule the island for a year.

Each year members of the clans competed in a race to get the first egg laid by a sooty tern that nested on a very small island near Easter Island. In springtime young men would climb down a 1000-foot cliff to the beach. Then they had to swim about one and a quarter miles through rough seas to the small island. There they waited, sometimes for weeks, for a sooty tern to land on the islet, build a nest, and lay eggs. The young man who found the first egg was the winner. He would swim back to the main island carrying the prized egg in his headband. The young man's master became Easter Island's new birdman and leader—Makemake's representative on earth.

- ◆ *Objective:* To learn about the Birdman Cult of Easter Island and other facts about the island

- ◆ *Time to Complete Activity:* 2–3 hours

- ◆ *Materials Needed:* Research materials, paper, pencil

Directions:

_____ Read as much as you can about the Birdman Cult, the geography, weather, birds, and anything else you can find out about Easter Island.

Try to put yourself in the place of one of the young men who risked his life to get a bird's egg so his master could become the birdman and his clan could rule the island for a year. What might the young man have thought, felt, seen, smelled, or heard as he climbed down the cliff and waited on the islet for the bird to come?

_____ Write a story about the birdman contest from the point of view of one of these young men.

Variation: *A small group could write a play based on one of the birdman contest stories and act it out. One way would be to have a narrator who speaks the thoughts of the young man from the story while the other players pantomime (act out without speaking) the parts of the young man, the master, and other islanders.*

Name _____

Date _____

Navigating by Observing Wave Patterns

Sometime in the late 300's, Polynesian sailors and their families set out in huge canoes and came across the Pacific Ocean to Easter Island, probably by accident. They developed a complex culture that included creating hundreds of giant statues that represented their ancestors.

Even though the original islanders came upon Easter Island by accident, they probably knew that there was an island somewhere nearby. Like most ancient Polynesian sailors, they were almost certainly very good at observing how wave patterns change when an island group is within about fifty miles.

◆ *Objective:* To observe how wave patterns change when an object is placed in water

◆ *Time to Complete Activity:* $\frac{1}{2}$ hour

◆ *Materials Needed:* A pan that is at least 12 by 12 inches and at least 3 inches deep, a piece of heavy white paper to fit in the bottom of the pan, cellophane or masking tape, a ruler, a small glass, water, a bright overhead light, paper, pencil

---

Directions:

_____ Tape the paper to the bottom of the pan. Be sure that all edges of the paper are taped down.

_____ Fill the pan with water and place the pan under a bright overhead light.

_____ Holding the ruler horizontally, make waves by moving the ruler up and down gently in the water along one side of the pan.

_____ Observe the pattern of the waves. Are they straight, curved, parallel?

_____ Take the ruler out of the water and allow the waves to settle down.

_____ Place the glass in the pan and again make waves with the ruler.

_____ Observe the wave pattern this time. Is there any change? If so, what is causing the change?

Variation: *Sketch the different wave patterns that you observe.*

Sketch an overhead view of a boat approaching an island and show wave patterns that might occur around the island.

     Wonders of World Cultures: Exploring Asia and Oceania

Name _____

Date _____

Making a Mini Moai

Sometime in the late 300's, Polynesian sailors and their families set out in huge canoes and came across the Pacific Ocean to Easter Island, probably by accident. They developed a complex culture that included creating hundreds of giant statues that represented their ancestors. The islanders call these statues *moai*.

With only stone tools, the Easter Islanders carved statues that weigh as much as 80 tons. Elaborate designs were carved into the statues, and some had headdresses and white eyes. Family groups (clans) on the island competed to build the largest and most splendid statues. A food shortage led to fighting among clans, and rival clans toppled one another's statues.

In modern times, archaeologists and others have come to Easter Island to find out some of its secrets. They have raised some of the statues and placed them on their original platforms.

- ◆ *Objective:* To carve a head in the shape of a moai

- ◆ *Time to Complete Activity:* 1 hour

- ◆ *Materials Needed:* Bar of soft soap (like Ivory™), felt-tip pen, utensil with a small scoop on one end, like a potato peeler

---

Directions:

_____ Using the drawing of the moai on this page as a guide, draw the outline of the face, including eyes, nose, mouth, and chin, on one side of the bar of soap. This will be your guide for making the head.

_____ Use the scoop to carefully remove bits of soap. First work on the front of the head, then the back, then one side, then the other, so you get an idea of how the whole head is coming along. The back of the moai is usually fairly flat.

_____ When the head has taken shape, start working on details like the mouth and eyes.

This moai, which now is in the British Museum, weighs four tons and is 8.25 feet tall. The back of the statue is covered with elaborate designs.

Name _____

Date _____

Thought/Discussion Questions

1. Since Easter Island was discovered by Europeans, writers and others have put forward some fantastic stories about how the huge statues were created. One writer proposed that aliens from outer space told earth dwellers to make these statues and many other monuments of ancient mankind, such as Stonehenge. Why do you think present-day humans suggest such stories, aside from wanting to be in the spotlight?

_____

_____

_____

_____

2. Archaeologists have found evidence that damage from rats reduced the number of trees on the island. Can you think of other ways that the Easter Islanders probably caused their forests to decline?

_____

_____

_____

_____

3. The Easter Islanders used up their resources, especially trees, and could not travel to other lands because they did not have boats large and strong enough to go very far out to sea. Eventually there was famine, the culture collapsed, and many people died. Some writers compare what happened on Easter Island with what is happening on our planet in the present time. Do you see any similarities?

_____

_____

_____

_____

SECTION 2

Cultural Wonders of Asia and Oceania

CHAPTER 3: **Rock Art Wonders of Australia**

Chapter Summary

What are the "wonders" in this story?

- The paintings and engravings found on rock surfaces, primarily in caves, that provide knowledge about the ancient culture of the Australian Aborigines.

What are the major themes covered in the story and activities in this chapter?

- Traditional Aborigine culture survived for thousands of years in Australia until the arrival of Europeans.

- The rock art of Australian Aborigines shows a world filled with opposing forces—those that work for the good of the society, such as the *wandjina* (the ancestors), and those who work for the downfall of the society, such as the mischievous and evil spirits.

- Aborigines have survived in Australia to the present day and still try to carry on some of their traditions.

Answers to "Think About It" Question

(page 29)

"The wet" in northern Australia is, as you would guess, the rainy or monsoon season, which lasts from January to March, summertime in the Southern Hemisphere. There is a lot of flooding during the monsoon season.

Answers to "Thought/Discussion Questions"

(page 33) 1. and 2. Answers will vary.

Bibliography

Adult books

Layton, Robert. *Australian Rock Art: A New Synthesis.* Cambridge: Cambridge University Press, 1992.

Morgan, S. *My Place.* New York: Seaver Books, 1987. (samples of Aboriginal English dialect)

Pilger, J. *A Secret Country: The Hidden Australia.* New York: Knopf, 1991.

Trezise, P. J. *Dream Road: A Journey of Discovery.* St. Leonard's, New South Wales: Allen & Unwin, 1993.

Juvenile books

Darian-Smith, K. *Exploration into Australia.* Parsippany, New York: New Discovery Books, 1995.

Holder, R. *Aborigines of Australia.* Vero Beach, Florida: Rourke Publications, 1987.

Meisel, J. *Australia: The Land Down Under.* New York: Benchmark Books, 1997.

Nile, R. *Australian Aborigines.* Austin, Texas: Raintree/Steck-Vaughn, 1993.

Magazine articles

Newman, Cathy. "The Uneasy Magic of Australia's Cape York Peninsula," *National Geographic.* Vol. 189, (June 1996), pp. 2–33.

CHAPTER 3:
Rock Art Wonders of Australia

Handprints made by Aborigines on walls of rock shelters in Australia announce, "I was here."

Source: The Native Tribes of Central Australia, by
Baldwin Spencer and F. J. Gillen. (London: Macmillan & Co., Ltd., 1899)

OCEANIA

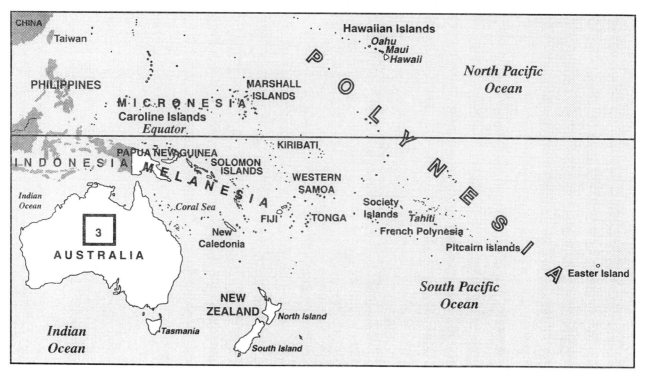

 The focus of this chapter is the rock art of northern and central Australia, which dates from about 20,000 years ago to the 1920's.

Map of Australia showing rock art areas mentioned in text.

Treasures of an Ancient Culture

If you were to go into a rock shelter in Australia, you might be surprised to find not just bare rock walls but a painting of a figure with bony ribs and insect-like antennae, footprints, handprints, animals with all the internal organs showing as if their skin were transparent, policemen with rifles, sailing ships, and men smoking pipes. These are some of the treasures of rock art of the Aborigine culture of Australia. The earliest rock paintings were made with human blood as long as 20,000 years ago, and the most recent ones were made with mineral paints in the 1920's.

Since contact with Indonesians and Europeans in the 1700's and 1800's, the Aboriginal lifestyle has changed. Now, the Aborigines do not paint on the walls of rock shelters, but there are a few areas of Australia (mainly in the northern and central regions) where elders still remember the meaning of the rock art and have passed their knowledge on to their children and to scientists.

Rock Art of the Ancestors

According to Aboriginal beliefs, the "Dreamtime" was when the land and social systems of the Aborigines were being created by heroic ancestors called *wandjina,* who did their work by walking back and forth, leaving "dreaming tracks."

As the wandjina walked around, they organized the Aboriginal world by placing tall stones in the bush and making rock formations to mark clan areas. They also created a social order called *wunan,* in which clans exchanged gifts and women in marriage.

Designs of the wandjina in human or animal form were used in body decorations and in the art that was painted or engraved on cave walls. The dreaming tracks were also painted on cave walls and in sand drawings.

The Dreamtime heroes gave each clan its own sacred places, such as water holes, rocks, and cave shelters. These places were filled with the sacred spirits of the great ancestors. Legends, songs, and dances tell how the sacred places were created.

The wandjina were part of the Aboriginal life cycle, from birth to death. The Aborigines believed that the wandjina placed the spirits of the clan's unborn children in the sacred water holes where men and women could come and get them when they wanted a baby. At death a clan member's bones were carried to a wandjina cave.

Each clan was responsible for repainting its wandjina rock art every year, usually at the start of the rainy season. The clans believed the wandjina would be sad if their rock art were not "freshened up."

Rock Art of the Hunt

While hunting and gathering food, Aborigines liked to keep a record of the animals and plants they found and ate by painting pictures of them on the walls of the rock shelters where they stayed during the rainy season.

Animal paintings were always done in the "X-ray" style. Internal organs—the heart, lungs, esophagus, stomach, intestines, eye nerve, backbone, ribs, and leg bones—were drawn in. Bark paintings done today by Aborigines look like these X-ray paintings.

Handprint stencils on rock shelters walls record that a person was there. Older people still visit caves where they left their stencils when they were young.

Rock Art Showing Mischievous and Evil Creatures

In contrast to the rock art of the wandjina, who brought order to the Aborigines, there is rock art that shows creatures who brought disorder and sometimes death. Many Aborigines believe these paintings were put in rock caves by the creatures themselves, to make fun of the wandjina, the ancestors.

X-ray animal

The least harmful of these creatures are the *mimi*. Sometimes they help and sometimes they don't.

In rock art the mimi have humanlike forms, with long, thin bodies. They are usually shown in movement and holding weapons.

According to Aboriginal beliefs, the mimi were the first to write songs, and they showed people how to hunt and cook kangaroo. But when angered, the mimi could punish people.

The Aborigines in Arnhem Land (see map of Australia) believe that the mimi still exist and live in nearby sandstone cliffs. It is said that at night the mimi can be heard moving around, making scuffling sounds with their feet. If someone approaches their cliff houses, he must call out to announce that he is there. Then the mimi will protect him from sickness.

The people of the Kimberleys (see map of Australia) believed in spirits called *wurrulu-wurrulu* and *nganjdjala-nganjdjala* who were sometimes helpful, sometimes harmful, and always unpredictable.

When people saw clouds rising from the ground after rain, they said that these spirits were ripening yams over a campfire, and that meant it would be a good year for finding yams.

The people believed the wurrulu-wurrulu stole wild honey.

Both of Kimberley spirit creatures were said to be small mischief-makers, with big heads and round cheeks. In rock shelter paintings they can be seen as small figures with upraised arms.

The *namurrudu* were supposedly very harmful. According to Aboriginal beliefs, they flew around at night and killed people, sometimes with lightning. Paintings of these evil creatures show them with clawlike hands and feet. Sometimes they were shown with clubs, which they used to stun their victims.

Namurrudu with string of fish

To keep Aboriginal children from wandering away from camp at night, people told stories about the namurrudu. One is about a namurrudu who went fishing. When he caught fish, he would thread them on a string, which he kept in the water. When his back was turned, someone stole some of his fish. To punish the thief, the creature followed him and his group back to the cave where they were spending the night. After they had settled down in the cave, the namurrudu plugged the cave entrance with a huge stone. The next morning no one came out of the cave. No child would want to meet that creature at night!

Probably the scariest figures that are shown in rock art are *Argula* and *Kakadja*.

Kakadja is said to steal children who cry at night. Older people tell children that if they won't stop crying, Kakadja, in the form of a huge invisible bird, will carry them off to his mother who will smash their heads against a stone. Birds who make mournful sounds in the night are said to be the souls of children killed by Kakadja who are still crying out to their mothers to come get them.

Argula, who is shown in rock art with long ears, is also used to scare children into obeying their parents. One story tells about a mother and her child who were out in the bush collecting wild honey. When the mother finished collecting the honey in her bark basket, she said to her child, "Come on." The child, who was licking up some spilled honey, said, "I'll catch up." He lagged behind. When his mother was out of sight, he suddenly heard a chopping sound and thought someone nearby had found another tree with a wild honeybee nest in it and was chopping it down. He went to investigate rather than catching up with his mother. The sound was made by the evil spirit Argula, in the form of a black giant, who was chopping down a tree. He grabbed the disobedient child and put him in his bucket. Argula ran with the child to his underground tunnel and prepared to cook and eat him. Just before the child was to be cooked a bat swooped down and saved him.

Rock Art After Contact with White Settlers

Many Aborigines did not survive their contact with white people. The natives were killed by European diseases and by police who saw them as a nuisance because they would not stay off the new settlers' land. Aborigines shared their lands freely with other clans for hunting and gathering purposes. They had no way of understanding the white settlers' idea of owning private land.

Rock art paintings of the 1700's and 1800's recorded the Aboriginal contact with outsiders. First came sailors from Indonesia. Rock paintings along the northern coast of Australia show Indonesian dugout canoes, which the Aborigines learned how to copy and used to travel between the mainland and nearby islands. The Indonesians did not come to Australia to stay; they just wanted to trade.

The British, however, came to stay. After their first contact with the British in 1788, Aborigine rock art started to show sailing ships, men on horseback, and pistols.

In the interior of Australia, where white men had cattle ranches, the Aborigine rock art shows white men wearing hats. Horses, guns, and cattle brands are also shown.

Traditional Art Today

Some Aborigines have found a way to carry on their traditional artwork and support their families.

They paint wandjina, spirits, and animals in the X-ray style. Images from the white man's culture, such as ships, rifles, and policemen, are not painted.

Young artists are learning from older ones how to create the style and body shapes that correctly represent the ancient beings. In this way, perhaps, the rock art traditions will be passed on to future generations, and knowledge about the unique culture of the Australian Aborigines will stay alive, instead of being remembered only in history books.

> **Think About It—**
>
> *Groups of Aborigines would go into caves during "the wet," as they called it (and still call it). What do you think this means?*

Sand Drawing

Aboriginal rock paintings picture tall, skinny humanlike figures, animals with their internal organs showing, footprints, handprints, sailing ships and many other subjects. The earliest rock paintings were made with human blood as long as 20,000 years ago, and the most recent ones were made with mineral paints in the 1920's.

Aborigines do not paint on the walls of rock shelters anymore, but there are a few areas of Australia, mainly in the northern and central regions, where elders still remember the meaning of the rock art and have passed their knowledge on to their children and to scientists.

Another form of artwork done by Aborigines, mainly women, is sand drawing. They still use sand drawings to illustrate legends about heroic ancestors as well as everyday stories. The drawings use simple designs, like circles and lines. For instance, a circle might stand for a sleeping person, or a semicircle could stand for a person sitting in the sand. The artists are also skilled at showing animal footprints by pressing the sand with different parts of their hands (see drawings below).

- ◆ *Objective:* To create a sand drawing
- ◆ *Time to Complete Activity:* 1–2 hours
- ◆ *Materials Needed:* A sandy area or a shallow container filled with sand, a piece of cardboard or a cookie sheet to smooth the sand, resource materials about animal tracks

---

Directions:

_____ In your sandy area or sandbox, copy the prints you see on this page.

_____ After doing some research about animal tracks, try to create the tracks of other animals, especially ones that are seen in Australia, like kangaroo, emu, and large lizards. (What would a lizard drag behind that would make a wavy pattern in the sand?)

Variation: *Illustrate a favorite folktale with designs in the sand. First, decide on simple designs that will stand for characters in the story. Decide how you will show movement and how you will change scenes in the story.*

Dog track

Make toe prints with tip of finger.

Make claw prints with fingernail.

Make pad of track with palm.

Wild Turkey Track

How would you make these shapes with your hand?

Name _____

Date _____

Making an X-Ray Bark Drawing

Aboriginal rock paintings picture tall, skinny humanlike figures, animals with their internal organs showing, footprints, handprints, sailing ships and many other subjects. The earliest rock paintings were made with human blood as long as 20,000 years ago, and the most recent ones were made with mineral paints in the 1920's.

Aborigines do not paint on rock shelter walls anymore, but some elders of the northern and central regions of Australia still remember the meaning of the rock paintings. They say that paintings of animals and plants on the walls of rock shelters were a way for the Aborigines to keep a record of the animals and plants they found and ate.

Animal paintings were always done in the "X-ray" style, showing their internal organs. The heart, lungs, esophagus, stomach, intestines, eye nerve, backbone, ribs, and leg bones were drawn in a very simplified way. Bark paintings done today by Aborigines look a lot like these X-ray paintings.

- ◆ *Objective:* To create an "X-ray" bark drawing

- ◆ *Time to Complete Activity:* 2–3 hours

- ◆ *Materials Needed:* Brown construction paper or brown wrapping paper (cut in rectangular shape) that will imitate bark, dark-red chalk or crayon to simulate the red-ocher mineral paint used in Aboriginal drawings, white chalk or white crayon, 2 thin branches of same length as shorter sides of paper, with leaves and small twigs removed, large needle, heavy-duty brown thread or embroidery floss, scissors, white practice paper, masking tape, pencil

---

Directions:

_____ Decide on the animal you want to draw and practice making X-ray drawings. As Aboriginal artists do, mark off sections of the body at major joints, like hips, ankles, and shoulders, and draw the internal organs in a simplified manner (see example below).

_____ Don't hesitate to add more lines and shapes if you think it would improve your artwork. Think about where you will use the red and where you will use the white colors in your final drawing.

_____ When you are finished practicing, re-create your design on the sheet of brown construction paper, using the red and white chalk (or crayons).

_____ Sew the thin branches onto the top and bottom edges of your drawing by simply pushing the thread through the edge of the paper and looping it around the branch. Tie off the ends of the thread and secure them on the back of the paper with small strips of masking tape.

X-ray style animal painting shows simplified internal organs and bones.

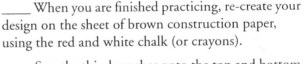

Name _____

Date _____

Creating a Cautionary Folktale

Aboriginal rock paintings picture tall, skinny humanlike figures, animals with their internal organs showing, footprints, handprints, sailing ships and many other subjects. The earliest rock paintings were made with human blood as long as 20,000 years ago, and the most recent ones were made with mineral paints in the 1920's.

Some of the rock paintings show creatures who are mischievous or evil. According to Aboriginal beliefs, these creatures brought disorder and sometimes death to people. The mischief-makers might steal honey or blankets when no one was looking, but the evil spirits would roam the bush looking for children to kill and eat.

To keep them quiet and teach them to obey their parents, children were told scary stories about the evil spirits pictured in the rock art.

One of these scary stories is about an evil spirit named Kakadja, who is said to steal children who cry at night. Older people tell children that if they won't stop crying, Kakadja, in the form of a huge invisible bird, will swoop down and carry them off to his horrible mother who will smash their heads against a stone. When a bird makes mournful cooing sounds at night, children are told that the sounds are made by the souls of children killed by Kakadja, who are still calling out to their mothers to come get them.

◆ *Objective:* To write a cautionary tale (a story that scares children somewhat and warns them against doing something they know they shouldn't do)

◆ *Time to Complete Activity:* 1–2 hours

◆ *Materials Needed:* Paper, pencil, resource materials

Directions:

_____ Ask your teacher or librarian to recommend some cautionary tales to read, like stories from the Brothers Grimm, Aesop's fables, and others.

_____ Write your own cautionary tale. It can be based on a story from your own childhood or something that you invent. You could also interview parents, grandparents, or friends for story ideas.

_____ Illustrate your stories.

Variation: *Have a classroom contest to see who can write the scariest story. Or read your stories to younger children who can vote on the one they think is scariest and most likely to keep them from doing something they shouldn't do. (Don't scare them too much!)*

Name _____

Date _____

Thought/Discussion Questions

1. If you were forced to live in a cave, or a series of caves, during the rainy season, what would you paint on the walls of the cave?

   _____

   _____

   _____

   _____

   _____

   _____

   _____

   _____

2. The Australian Aborigines do not have a written language. One of the ways they pass on knowledge about their culture is through stories and songs. Does your culture pass on knowledge by telling stories and singing songs? If not, how is information passed on?

   _____

   _____

   _____

   _____

   _____

   _____

   _____

   _____

CHAPTER 4: *Wonders in the Pits—Emperor Ch'in Shih Huang Ti's Warriors*

Chapter Summary

What are the "wonders" in this story?

- The clay soldiers buried in the third century B.C. in what is now central China provide a treasure of information about Chinese civilization during the rule of Ch'in Shih Huang Ti, the first emperor of China.

What are the major themes covered in the story and activities in this chapter?

- The first emperor of China, Ch'in Shih Huang Ti, was a powerful ruler who commanded workers to construct a burial mound and pits containing thousands of life-size clay representations of guardian soldiers, horses, and chariots.
- The region of Ch'in had a powerful military organization that Ch'in Shih Huang Ti used to conquer all the other regions of China, unifying China in the process.
- Because Ch'in Shih Huang Ti was afraid of death and defeat, he had his subjects build part of the Great Wall to keep out barbarian tribes in the north, and pits and a clay army to protect his tomb from attack by grave robbers and others.

Answers to "Think About It" Question

(page 39)

As the supreme ruler of China, Ch'in Shih Huang Ti punished citizens harshly for breaking laws. He also forced thousands of his subjects to work in extremely difficult conditions to build the Great Wall of China. While the citizens of China suffered, he lived in luxury in 300 palaces with beautiful gardens. He possessed jade and other precious jewels. He also used his country's resources to build a tomb and had thousands of clay soldiers made to guard the tomb after his death.

After Ch'in Shih Huang Ti died, the citizens rebelled. A new regime was started under the Han emperors.

Activity "The Legends of Ch'in Shih Huang Ti and the Great Wall"

(page 42)

If you would like to extend this activity, here is how the story ends, according to legend:

If she cut her finger and let her blood drip on the bones, the gods told her, she would know which bones were those of her husband. When Meng Chiang-nu did this, she saw that her blood soaked into some of the bones and not others. She knew then that the blood-soaked bones were those of her dead husband.

As she was gathering up the bones to carry them back home for burial, the emperor happened to come by. He immediately fell in love with her and demanded that she become one of his wives. She knew that she could not refuse the emperor, so Meng Chiang-nu agreed. Determined to mourn and bury her husband correctly, she asked the emperor if she could wait 100 days before marrying him. He agreed on the condition that she sew and embroider a gown for him to wear. This she did, but when the emperor saw the finished gown, he was so astonished at its beauty that he went back on his promise and commanded her to become his wife immediately.

Meng Chiang-nu delayed again by asking the emperor if her husband could be given an official state funeral beside the sea. The emperor agreed, but during the funeral the grieving widow threw herself into the sea to join the soul of her dead husband.

The emperor was furious but amazed at the same time that Meng Chiang-nu's love for her husband was so strong that she would kill herself to try to be with him again. The emperor had a monument to Meng Chiang-nu erected on the coast, overlooking the sea.

Answers to "Thought/Discussion Questions"

(page 43) 1–3. Answers will vary.

Bibliography

Adult books

Cottrell, Leonard. *The Tiger of Ch'in*. New York: Holt, Rinehart, 1962.

Fryer, Jonathan. *The Great Wall of China*. London: New English Library, 1975.

Götze, Heinz, ed. *Chinese and Japanese Calligraphy Spanning Two Thousand Years*. New York: Prestel-Verlag, 1989.

Murowchick, Robert E., ed. *Cradles of Civilization: China*. Norman, Oklahoma: University of Oklahoma Press, 1994.

Temple, Robert. *The Genius of China: 3,000 Years of Science, Discovery, and Invention*. New York: Simon & Schuster, 1986.

Lo, Che-wen. *The Great Wall*. New York: McGraw-Hill, 1981.

Juvenile books

Lazo, Caroline. *The Terra Cotta Army of Emperor Q'in*. New York: New Discovery, 1993.

Waterlow, Julia. *The Ancient Chinese*. New York: Thomson Learning, 1994.

Magazine articles

Mazzatenta, O. Louis. "China's Warriors Rise from the Earth," *National Geographic*, Vol. 190, (October 1996), pp. 68–85.

CHAPTER 4:
Wonders in the Pits—Emperor Ch'in Shih Huang Ti's Warriors

Passageway through Great Wall of China, built by Ch'in Shih Huang Ti and other rulers of China.

This illustration and illustration on p. 42 from A Cycle of Cathay or China, South and North with Personal Reminiscences, *by W. A. P. Martin. (New York: Fleming H. Revell Company, 1896)*

ASIA

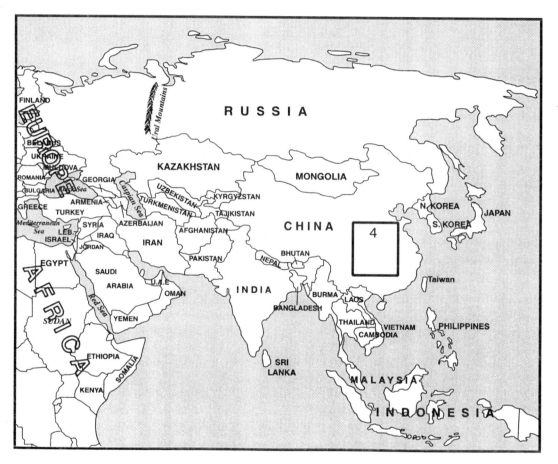

④ This chapter focuses on the life of the first emperor of China, Ch'in Shih Huang Ti, during his rule from 221 to 210 or 209 B.C.

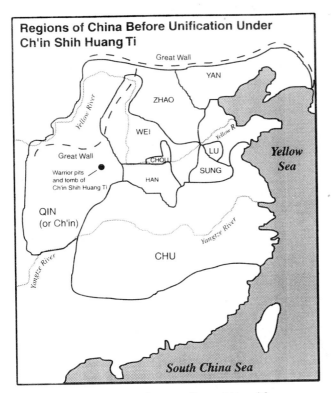

Regions of China Before Unification Under Ch'in Shih Huang Ti

Great Wall

YAN

ZHAO

WEI

Great Wall

Yellow River

LU

CHO

SUNG

Yellow Sea

Warrior pits and tomb of Ch'in Shih Huang Ti

HAN

QIN (or Ch'in)

Yangtze River

CHU

Yangtze River

South China Sea

Clay figures tell a story of power, military might, and fear of defeat and death.

Wonders in the Pits

In 1974, farmers near the town of Xian, in central China, were digging a well. It is not known if they found water, but they did find life-size clay heads, which they gave to the grandmother of their family. She placed the heads on her mantel and worshiped them as gods.

An archaeologist named Yuan Zhongyi heard about the heads found in the well shaft. He came to the farmer's field, set up his tent, and began to investigate the area around the well. Zhongyi and other archaeologists discovered the outline of a pit and started excavating clay figures that they found buried there. Within several years, three other pits were found, one of them empty. The pits are about three quarters of a mile from the tomb mound of the first emperor of China, Ch'in Shih Huang Ti.

Little by little, one brush stroke at a time, archaeologists have uncovered a treasure of Chinese history. They think that about 8,000 life-size clay soldiers, horses, and chariots were buried in the pits. These are the guardians of Ch'in Shih Huang Ti's tomb. Originally, they stood shoulder to shoulder, real weapons in hand, ready to fight off anyone who would dare to invade the great emperor's tomb.

Soon after the emperor died, rebels burned the pine roof covering the clay army. The roof caved in during the fire, toppling and burying the soldiers.

Only a small portion of the army has been dug up so far. Eventually, the whole army will be put back together, and the emperor's tomb may even be reopened. Who knows what treasures archaeologists will find there?

The King of Ch'in

The man who was powerful enough to command workers to make thousands of life-size clay soldiers to guard his tomb started out with the name Cheng. He became the king of the region of Ch'in (or Qin, see map above) at the tender age of thirteen, in 246 B.C. At the time, China was not unified but was made up of many individual regions that constantly fought with one another.

The Military Machine of Ch'in

When Cheng became the king of Ch'in, the region's military force was already strong and well disciplined. Terror was one of their most effective weapons. Chinese historians reported that the army of the neighboring region of Zhao was starved into surrendering, then all 400,000 Zhao soldiers were slaughtered. According to one historian, the Ch'in army moved across the land, devouring the regions of China like a silkworm devours a mulberry leaf.

Archaeologists have dug up enough of Shih Huang Ti's clay soldiers to see how the Ch'in army fought battles. In Pit 1, archers form the front ranks.

They wore light armor, and each man carried a bagful of arrows on his back. The clay figures also carried real weapons of battle—bows and crossbows. The crossbow was an advanced weapon that could pierce an enemy's armor.

Behind the archers came the infantry (foot soldiers) and the chariots. The infantry carried weapons for close-in fighting—dagger, lance, and battle-ax. Men riding in the chariots carried bows and crossbows for long-range fighting and lances for close-in fighting.

Smaller units of foot soldiers protected the sides and rear of the army.

In Pit 2, the fighting group was made up of archers, chariots, and cavalry (men on horseback). The cavalry was equipped with crossbows and halberds (combination ax and spike).

Guards armed only with spears were found in Pit 3. Possibly, they guarded the officers who commanded the army and performed ceremonial duties.

The Great Wall of China

First Emperor of China

Twenty years after he became ruler of Ch'in, Cheng directed his military machine to conquer all of the other regions of China. After they had done so, when he was thirty-eight years old, he gave himself the grand name of Shih Huang Ti, which means First Sovereign Emperor. He was truly the first emperor of a defeated, but united, China.

Shih Huang Ti controlled his empire as the supreme human authority. No one was supposed to oppose him, but at least three men tried to assassinate him. Perhaps because of these attempts on his life, he was constantly afraid of death and defeat. It was said that he slept in a different room of the palace each night so that no one would know where he was.

Shih Huang Ti feared the unknown and defeat by the barbarian tribes of the north, so he ordered a large section of the Great Wall to be built between 224 and 210 B.C. Five hundred miles of the wall were completed in the last year alone.

Peasants and ex-soldiers by the hundreds of thousands were forced to labor on the wall. Many died from working in extreme cold with little food or shelter. The wall was called "the longest cemetery on earth" because so many workers died on the job and were buried inside it.

Eventually, the wall stretched 4,000 miles across the northern part of China. It was mostly made up of sections built by former kings of other regions.

Building his tomb, with its thousands of guardian "soldiers" was also a way for Shih Huang Ti to protect himself, even in the afterlife, against defeat by unknown outside forces. He was also afraid of grave robbers. He commanded that automatic crossbows be set up to fire on anyone who might break into the tomb pits. However, thieves did manage to get in and steal many of the weapons that had been placed in the clay soldiers' hands.

Toward the end of his life Shih Huang Ti spent most of his time looking for a way to live forever. He believed the stories of a magician who told him there were magic mountains in the eastern sea. One taste of a fungus that grew on these mountains would give everlasting life, according to the magician. It was on a trip in 210 B.C. to find a life-extending potion that the emperor died.

Treasures of Art

Not only are the clay statues of soldiers, horses, and chariots, priceless sources of information about the military machine and the first emperor of China, they are also works of art.

Each statue of both men and horses has individual features. Perhaps they were modeled after actual soldiers and horses in the emperor's army. For instance, one soldier has a scowl on his face and a broad, flat nose. Another soldier has a high forehead, a sharp nose, and a slight smile on his lips.

The clothing and armor worn by the clay soldiers is also very realistic. For instance, the plates of armor on the chest are fixed, but the plates on the shoulders are flexible, to allow arm movement. Generals wear tassels and other decorations to show their status.

The hairstyles and head coverings show different ranks and jobs. Archers wore their long hair braided and tied in a bun to the right side. Cavalry soldiers wore their hair braided under a cap that tied around the chin. Generals wore hats that look like stiff cloth napkins.

Paint that remains on the statues show that originally they were painted with bright colors. One general had a black robe over a red undergarment, blue padded leggings, and a black hat with red ties.

Treasures Yet to be Found

Archaeologists can only guess at what will be found inside the emperor's huge burial mound. According to Chinese historical records, it may contain a model of one of Shih Huang Ti's 300 palaces, the beautiful gardens he built around the palaces, jade and other precious jewels, and even miniature rivers representing the great waterways of China—the Yellow and Yangtze rivers.

Certainly Ch'in Shih Huang Ti failed in his attempt to find a way to live forever, but the remains of his clay army and whatever is found in his tomb will provide knowledge about ancient China that will last forever.

Think About It—

Looking back over the chapter, can you think of some of the reasons that Ch'in Shih Huang Ti's dynasty was overthrown soon after he died?

The clay statues show some of the elaborate hairstyles and "caps" of the emperor's soldiers. The figure on the left is a general.

Name _____

Date _____

The Art of Chinese Calligraphy

The first emperor of China, Ch'in Shih Huang Ti, who ruled from 221 to 210 B.C., used his powerful army to conquer and unify all the regions of China.

To encourage people to think of themselves as Chinese rather than as citizens of individual regions, Ch'in Shih Huang Ti decided that everyone would use the same round coins as money instead of the shovel-shaped, knife-shaped, and other kinds of coins that they had been using. He also commanded that everybody use the same weights and measures for doing business.

To make sure that all educated people in China could read one another's writing, Ch'in Shih Huang

Ti directed his minister Li Si to create a standard way of writing Chinese characters and to assign standard meanings to the characters.

Chinese writing is picture writing. Each character represents something (as shown below). On the other hand, the individual letters of Western alphabets (*a, b, c . . .*) do not mean anything by themselves. They have to be put together to make words.

Writing Chinese characters is an everyday activity, but it is also an art form called *calligraphy,* which has been practiced for thousands of years. Artists study the work of the great masters of calligraphy and spend many years practicing. Eventually, they develop their own personal style of writing.

- ◆ *Objective:* To practice writing Chinese characters and create a hanging scroll

- ◆ *Time to Complete Activity:* 1 hour

- ◆ *Materials Needed:* Small paintbrush with tapered point, 4 by 11 inch card stock (like index card paper), practice paper, India ink (or black tempera paint), dish, hole punch, string or monofilament, scissors, pencil, ruler, book with Chinese characters

---

Directions:

_____ Pour a small amount of India ink (or black tempera mixed with a small amount of water) in a dish.

_____ Draw a very faint line down the middle of the practice paper. Practice painting the characters you see on this page or copy characters from a book. Center your characters on the line. Dip just the tip of the brush in the ink and wipe off excess ink on the side of the dish before you paint.

bird

sheep

tree

sun

_____ When you're ready, make your final painting on the card stock, after drawing a faint guideline down the center of the paper.

_____ Punch two holes in the top edge of your "scroll."

_____ Cut a piece of string or monofilament and tie the ends through the holes so you can hang your "scroll."

Variation: *Invite someone to your classroom who can write in Chinese. Ask him or her to write a Chinese poem or saying and use that as the writing that you copy for your scroll.*

Making a Classroom Museum of Money

The first emperor of China, Ch'in Shih Huang Ti, who ruled from 221 to 210 B.C., used his powerful army to conquer and unify all the regions of China.

To encourage people to think of themselves as Chinese rather than as citizens of individual regions, Ch'in Shih Huang Ti decided that everyone would use the same round coins as money, instead of the shovel-shaped, knife-shaped, and other kinds of money that were used in different regions.

The round coins had a square hole in the middle so they could be strung together on a string, which made them easier to carry. China's system of money stayed basically the same for the next 2,000 years.

◆ *Objective:* To learn about the history of money systems

◆ *Time to Complete Activity:* 4–5 hours, over a period of several days

◆ *Materials Needed:* Poster board, markers, index cards, tape, glue, world maps, research materials

---

Directions:

_____ Read as much as you can about the history of money.

_____ Make a History of Money "museum" in your classroom. In the museum, try to present answers to the following questions. Include examples.

- What is **bartering**?
- Why was bartering no longer used in developing societies?
- What were some of the earliest types of money before coins? Show the area of the world where this early money was used.
- What qualities does money need to be useful? (One quality money needs is to be accepted by everyone in the society.)
- What led to the invention of coins? What did some of the first coins look like?

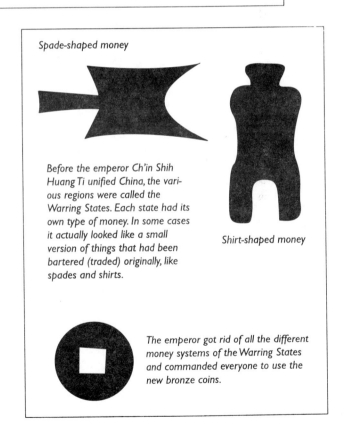

Spade-shaped money

Before the emperor Ch'in Shih Huang Ti unified China, the various regions were called the Warring States. Each state had its own type of money. In some cases it actually looked like a small version of things that had been bartered (traded) originally, like spades and shirts.

Shirt-shaped money

The emperor got rid of all the different money systems of the Warring States and commanded everyone to use the new bronze coins.

The Legends of Ch'in Shih Huang Ti and the Great Wall

The first emperor of China, Ch'in Shih Huang Ti, who ruled from 221 to 210 B.C., used his powerful army to conquer and unify all the regions of China. Archaeologists found a treasure of information about the emperor's army when they discovered pits filled with thousands of life-size clay statues of soldiers, horses, and chariots. This clay army was intended to protect the nearby tomb of the emperor.

Ch'in Shih Huang Ti was a very powerful, cruel ruler who forced hundreds of thousands of peasants and ex-soldiers to work in extremely harsh conditions to build sections of the Great Wall of China. The Great Wall, which extended across the northern frontier, was meant to keep out barbarian tribes.

Over the centuries, stories about the larger-than-life powers of the first emperor of China were recorded. One story tells of a magic whip that the emperor used to move a mountain range so workers could build the Great Wall. Another says the emperor commanded the wall to be built in one day!

Some of the stories, like the one below, tell of the hardship and suffering that Ch'in Shih Huang Ti caused during the building of the Great Wall.

The Story of Meng Chiang-nu

(in brief outline form)

Meng Chiang-nu was a teenage girl who married a young man of only sixteen.

When the emperor ordered construction of the Great Wall, Meng Chiang-nu's husband and many others were forced to leave home and travel a long distance to work on it.

The husband was treated very harshly and soon died. Like many others, he was buried in the wall.

At home, Meng Chiang-nu anxiously waited for news about her husband.

One winter night, she dreamed that her husband's spirit came to her and said he was freezing to death. He begged her for some warm clothes. Then suddenly, the spirit told her it was too late: He had already died and was buried in the wall.

The next morning, Meng Chiang-nu packed some winter clothing and set out to find her husband, hoping that he had not already died.

After a long and difficult trip, Meng Chiang-nu arrived at the Great Wall. She ran up and down the Wall, asking for information about her husband. One of the workmen said he was dead.

That night Meng Chiang-nu was visited again by the spirit of her husband. The spirit praised her for being such a loyal wife and promised never to forget her. She woke up and started crying.

The gods took pity on Meng Chiang-nu and caused a section of the Great Wall to crumble, exposing the bones of thousands of workers who died at the wall and were buried in it. Meng Chiang-nu wondered how she would find the remains of her husband among the jumble of bones.

- *Objective:* To stretch your imagination in a creative writing experience
- *Time to Complete Activity:* 1–2 hours
- *Materials Needed:* Resource materials, paper, pencil/pen

Directions:

_____ Read as much as you can about the climate of China, especially during the winter. Also, read about building the Great Wall of China.

_____ Write a poem or story based on the outline above. Write your own ending to the story.

Thought/Discussion Questions

1. Do you think Ch'in Shih Huang Ti believed in an afterlife? Please explain.

_____

_____

_____

_____

_____

2. Fantastic stories (legends) were told about the powers of Ch'in Shih Huang Ti. For instance, it was said that he commanded a magic horse to travel up to 300 miles a day. Every place the horse's hooves touched the ground a watchtower on the Great Wall sprang up. It was even reported that the emperor had commanded the wall to be built in one day! Can you think of any larger-than-life stories that are told about people in American history?

_____

_____

_____

_____

3. With his powerful army, Ch'in Shih Huang Ti forced all the regions of China to come under his control. He tried to unify China further by commanding that all citizens use the same kind of money and the same ways to weigh and measure things. Can you think of any other ways that a ruler could unify a country?

_____

_____

_____

_____

CHAPTER 5: *The Temple Wonders of Angkor*

Chapter Summary

What are the "wonders" in this story?

- The temples of Angkor (now in Cambodia) provide a treasure of information about the civilization of Angkor, which thrived in the Middle Ages.

What are the major themes covered in the story and activities in this chapter?

- The kings of Angkor built great stone temples to

secure their gods' protection for the Khmer people and their civilization.

- Khmer craftsmen were master stonecutters who carved many religious scenes and scenes from everyday life on the temple walls at Angkor.

- Angkor was a religious center and also the bustling central city of the Khmer civilization.

Answers to "Think About It" Question

(page 47) The Tonle Sap lake provided a lot of food for the people of Angkor.

Answers to "Using Sanskrit Numbers"

(page 51)

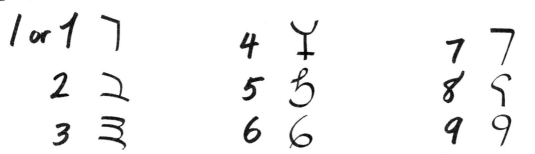

Answers to "Thought/Discussion Questions"

(page 54)

1. India—Sanskrit and Hinduism both came from India.

2. Answers will vary.

3. Answers will vary.

Bibliography

Adult books

Freeman, Michael, and Roger Warner. *Angkor: The Hidden Glories.* Boston: Houghton Mifflin, 1990.

Giteau, Madeleine. *The Civilization of Angkor.* New York: Rizzoli, 1976.

Mannikka, Eleanor. *Angkor Wat: Time, Space, and Kingship.* Honolulu: University of Hawaii Press, 1996.

Juvenile books

Chandler, David P. *The Land & People of Cambodia.* New York: HarperCollins, 1991.

Greenblatt, Miriam. *Enchantment of the World: Cambodia.* Chicago: Children's Press, 1995.

Sheehan, Sean. *Cambodia.* New York: Marshall Cavendish, 1996.

Cambodia in Pictures. Minneapolis: Lerner, 1996.

Magazine articles

Hornik, Richard. "The Battle of Angkor," *Time,* Vol. 139 (April 6, 1992), pp. 70–72.

CHAPTER 5:
The Temple Wonders of Angkor

One of the five gates leading into Angkor Thom, the main city area of Angkor.
(Illustration: Dover Publications, Inc.)

ASIA

This chapter focuses on the kingdom of Angkor (present-day Cambodia) from the end of the ninth century to the middle of the thirteenth century.

Treasures of Stone

Before 1800, Westerners did not believe travelers who came back from Cambodia with fantastic-sounding stories about ruins of mysterious abandoned temples in the hot, swampy jungle.

In 1860, a French naturalist named Henri Mouhot decided to search for the abandoned temples. After a month of slogging through the jungle along a crude road, Mouhot and his companions came to a clearing and a large rectangular pool. Further on, they came to a huge temple, *Angkor Wat.* ("Wat" means temple.) Mouhot also discovered the ruins of a great walled city, *Angkor Thom,* and hundreds of temples and monuments within a forty-square-mile area.

Through the years Buddhist monks had been praying at Angkor Wat, and they kept the jungle plants from taking over the temple. But other structures at Angkor were not so lucky. "Strangler fig" trees sent their huge roots into every opening, eventually pushing and pulling apart even the heaviest stone walls and temples. Much of Angkor was a jumble of broken walls, toppled statues, and fallen towers.

Unfortunately, Mouhot died of fever in 1861. He had not lived long enough to find out who built Angkor and when.

The same year that Mouhot died, the French took over the city of Saigon, in Cochin China (the southern part of present-day Vietnam). By 1887 they were in control of Cambodia, including Angkor. For decades French archaeologists and Khmer assistants carefully cut away the jungle vines and cleaned the stones of Angkor. The Khmer are the descendants of the people who built Angkor.

Unfortunately, gold, silver, or bronze treasures that were originally inside Angkor had been stolen years before. But the carvings and writings on the city's stone walls and monuments eventually provided a treasure of information about who built Angkor, when it was built, and the people who lived there.

Highly skilled craftsmen carved scenes in the outer and inner walls of Angkor. In addition to religious scenes, the carvings shows events in the lives of people of all classes, from peasants to kings.

Reports of visitors to Angkor when it was the capital of a great civilization are another source of information.

The Rulers Who Built Angkor

Archaeologists believe that from the end of the ninth century to the middle of the thirteenth century, the rulers at Angkor tried to create a perfect holy city by building religious temples containing statues and carvings of the gods and their stories. The rulers hoped that these religious symbols would please the gods who would then protect the city from foreign invasion, sickness, and other dangers that lurked in the jungle.

Yasovarman I. This king was the founder of Angkor in about 889. His favorite Hindu god was *Siva*. To please this god Yasovarman I built a stone temple that had sixty little chapels on its steps and five large shrines on the top. These five shrines represent the five peaks of Mount Meru, where the thirty-three Hindu gods live and are said to watch the stars rotate through the sky.

The capital city, called *Angkor Thom*, was built around the temple to Siva, but none of the wooden buildings of the city have survived.

Udayadityavarman II. This ruler's father, Suryavarman I, came to power in about 1010, after a civil war. Both father and son were determined to bring the country back from the troubles of civil war. Udayadityavarman built a temple called the *Baphuon*, described in inscriptions as being covered in gold and "shining with celestial brilliance" in order to please the gods.

Suryavarman II. In the mid-twelfth century, Suryavarman II built Angkor Wat, a temple to his favorite Hindu god, *Vishnu*. The world's largest temple, it covers 500 acres and measures more than half a mile on each side. Around the outside of the temple is a wide, water-filled border—a moat. A three-story pyramid base supports five huge shrines with towers reaching toward the sky. The shrines are connected by hallways. Carvings along the walls of the hallways tell the story of two armies fighting bloody battles.

Jayavarman VII. In 1177 Angkor Thom's protection was not strong enough to keep out the Cham of central Vietnam, who conquered the Khmer forces and took away most of the riches of the city. They did not destroy the temples, however.

A few years later, a new Khmer ruler named Jayavarman VII drove out the Cham. He decided the city needed more protection, so he continued building temples and strong walls around the city.

The walls built around Angkor Thom were more than a mile and a half long on each side. Chou Ta-kuan, a thirteenth-century Chinese traveler to Angkor, reported, "Outside the wall is a large ditch; outside the ditch, approach roads with large bridges. On either side of the bridge there are 54 stone guardians like stone generals, gigantic and terrible."

To please the gods, Jayavarman restored the Hindu temples and continued the carving of Hindu gods and their stories, even though he practiced the religion of Buddhism.

Each of the 51 towers of the temple called the Bayon has 4 human faces carved into it. Illustrations on pp. 48, 49, and 50 from The Straits of Malacca, Indo-China, and China; or, Ten Years' Travels, Adventures, and Residence Abroad, by J. Thomson, Harper & Brothers, Publishers. New York: 1875.

Inside the holy city, Jayavarman built a Buddhist temple called the *Bayon*. A statue of the Buddha, the central figure of Buddhism, originally stood in the center of the temple. Fifty-one chapels radiated out from the center, creating a lotus flower design, which is an important symbol in Buddhism. Each chapel has a tower with four huge human faces carved into it. Perhaps these carvings were meant to provide strong protection for the city.

The Life of the City (Angkor Thom)

The Marketplace. In the hallways of the Bayon you can see carvings that show how the

Wonders of World Cultures: Exploring Asia and Oceania

ordinary citizens of Angkor lived. The center of activity was the marketplace. All around it were workshops of craftsmen—including carpenters, cooks, bakers, goldsmiths, bronze smiths, and weavers. A cook can be seen dropping a little pig into a hot kettle of water, a goldsmith engraves a leaf design on a piece of jewelry, and a carpenter is using an ax with a long handle to cut the end of a tree trunk.

Continuing down the hallway, you can see carvings that show food and drink available at the market. A woman squats beside a pile of fish for sale. Another customer is buying vegetables. Another woman naps beside the basket of fruit she brought to the market while a girl attempts to reach over her and steal a piece of fruit.

The marketplace was alive with many other activities. The carvings show bystanders staring at people who are quarreling and shouting at each other. In another scene a cockfight is about to take place; owners hold back their fighting roosters while people make bets.

Lives of Nobles and Other Rich People.

None of the wooden houses where people of the upper classes lived have survived, but the Chinese visitor, Chou Ta-kuan, wrote that the houses of the nobles were large, with tile-covered roofs. People of the lower classes lived in smaller dwellings with roofs made of plant stalks and fronds, called thatch roofs.

Carvings in the Bayon show guards armed with stakes standing outside the house of a nobleman. The house is built of wood. On the upper floor is a porch where people could sit to catch a cool breeze.

Other carvings show men arriving at a feast. The nobleman sits on his heels and greets his guests by clasping their hands. An awning has been set up to provide shade in a garden. Guests sit on mats under the awning while servants bring dishes of food.

Many activities performed by servants are also shown in carvings. Cutting wood, bringing in jars of food, serving guests, cleaning pots and pans, and helping ladies with their hair and clothing were some of their duties.

Angkorians did not sew their clothes. Instead, they took long strips of cloth and wrapped them around their bodies. One lady can be seen in the carvings standing straight for her maids to wrap her "skirt." She seems to glance at herself in the mirror and smiles at what she sees.

Dancers were carved into temple walls. A few fragments of gold ornaments have been found at Angkor, showing that the dancers actually wore the huge hair decorations shown in carvings.

The carvings of dancing women, called *devata*, found on temples all over Angkor, suggest how the high-born ladies probably wore their hair.

Hair was kept in place by a metal net, by bringing braids together into one large bun, or by combing the hair over a support that framed the face. Sometimes gold thread was braided into the hair of Angkorian ladies.

Lives of the King and His Family.

The royal palace was made of wood, so no trace of it survives. Stone carvings show the king out on a balcony of the palace where he could be seen by the citizens of Angkor. Chou Ta-kuan reported that he had seen the king and his first wife sitting at a golden window of the king's private apartment.

The carvings also show the king either going off to war or to visit an outlying town, riding on his elephant. He was not supposed to leave Angkor, so he places objects on his throne to stand in for him—his bows and arrows, fans, and cups.

Stone carvings show armies going to war.

Inscriptions give some idea of the duties and responsibilities of the kings. In one inscription, King Rajendravarman reminds future kings that they have a sacred duty to protect the earth because they have conquered it.

Carved in a hallway of the temple of Angkor Wat is a magnificent scene that pictures the army of Surya-varman II going to war. It is like a parade, with columns of soldiers marching along carrying lances or bows and arrows. Leaders ride brightly painted elephants. Next comes the band, with trumpets blaring and drums beating. Clowns follow, then a somber group of Hindu religious men. A royal guard marches before the king, who is standing upright on his elephant. He looks back over the troops that follow him. Nothing, however, is known about how the Khmer fought battles, except for a scene at Angkor Wat that shows hand-to-hand fighting.

Inscriptions give the names of some of the kings' wives. Each king had many wives, but only the first wife shared her husband's successes and glory. A woman named Indradevi wrote about some of the things her sister Jayarajadevi had to do to help her husband, the king. She endured strict punishments while the king was away at war, in the hope that the gods would be pleased with her sacrifice and bring victories for the Khmer army. Indradevi does not detail the punishments, but says that her sister passed

"through the fire of torments and the sea of sorrows." The king came back victorious, but soon after he returned, his wife "entered nirvana" (died).

Lives of the Monks. Inscriptions on stone slabs found in the temples give us some idea about how these religious men lived. King Yasovarman I built a temple to the Hindu god *Vishnu*, one of the gods that was worshiped by the Khmer people. He wrote that he expected the monks who lived in the temple to be only interested in pursuing good conduct and study and to be satisfied with one meal a day. He limited their possessions to "three toothpicks, a portion of husked rice, forty leaves of betel and six arec nuts, and a bundle of firewood."

Monks were expected to perform religious ceremonies. For instance, when a new statue of a god was delivered to the temple, the monks would sprinkle the statue with water and perform the "opening of the eyes" ceremony by engraving pupils on the eyes. This would assure that the god lived in the statue.

The monks' way of life and the ceremonies they performed were meant to please the gods in return for the gods' protection of the city of Angkor and the civilization of the Khmer people.

Angkor Today

After a long decline, perhaps because of sickness or because of fighting for the throne among royal family members, Angkor was captured by an army from Thailand in 1431. The Khmers abandoned Angkor and moved their capital to Phnom Penh.

Where a thriving city once stood and where thousands of people went about their daily lives, now only two Buddhist monasteries exist inside the gates of Angkor Wat.

Throughout the centuries, pilgrims have continued coming to worship at Angkor Wat. Today, tourists also come to glimpse the remains of a glorious civilization. They enjoy walking the stones of the long main entrance to the temple, which seems like a pathway to the gods, and they come to watch the sun rise over the shrines soaring skyward.

ordinary citizens of Angkor lived. The center of activity was the marketplace. All around it were workshops of craftsmen—including carpenters, cooks, bakers, goldsmiths, bronze smiths, and weavers. A cook can be seen dropping a little pig into a hot kettle of water, a goldsmith engraves a leaf design on a piece of jewelry, and a carpenter is using an ax with a long handle to cut the end of a tree trunk.

Continuing down the hallway, you can see carvings that show food and drink available at the market. A woman squats beside a pile of fish for sale. Another customer is buying vegetables. Another woman naps beside the basket of fruit she brought to the market while a girl attempts to reach over her and steal a piece of fruit.

The marketplace was alive with many other activities. The carvings show bystanders staring at people who are quarreling and shouting at each other. In another scene a cockfight is about to take place; owners hold back their fighting roosters while people make bets.

Lives of Nobles and Other Rich People.
None of the wooden houses where people of the upper classes lived have survived, but the Chinese visitor, Chou Ta-kuan, wrote that the houses of the nobles were large, with tile-covered roofs. People of the lower classes lived in smaller dwellings with roofs made of plant stalks and fronds, called thatch roofs.

Carvings in the Bayon show guards armed with stakes standing outside the house of a nobleman. The house is built of wood. On the upper floor is a porch where people could sit to catch a cool breeze.

Other carvings show men arriving at a feast. The nobleman sits on his heels and greets his guests by clasping their hands. An awning has been set up to provide shade in a garden. Guests sit on mats under the awning while servants bring dishes of food.

Many activities performed by servants are also shown in carvings. Cutting wood, bringing in jars of food, serving guests, cleaning pots and pans, and helping ladies with their hair and clothing were some of their duties.

Angkorians did not sew their clothes. Instead, they took long strips of cloth and wrapped them around their bodies. One lady can be seen in the carvings standing straight for her maids to wrap her "skirt." She seems to glance at herself in the mirror and smiles at what she sees.

Dancers were carved into temple walls. A few fragments of gold ornaments have been found at Angkor, showing that the dancers actually wore the huge hair decorations shown in carvings.

The carvings of dancing women, called *devata*, found on temples all over Angkor, suggest how the high-born ladies probably wore their hair.

Hair was kept in place by a metal net, by bringing braids together into one large bun, or by combing the hair over a support that framed the face. Sometimes gold thread was braided into the hair of Angkorian ladies.

Lives of the King and His Family.
The royal palace was made of wood, so no trace of it survives. Stone carvings show the king out on a balcony of the palace where he could be seen by the citizens of Angkor. Chou Ta-kuan reported that he had seen the king and his first wife sitting at a golden window of the king's private apartment.

The carvings also show the king either going off to war or to visit an outlying town, riding on his elephant. He was not supposed to leave Angkor, so he places objects on his throne to stand in for him—his bows and arrows, fans, and cups.

Stone carvings show armies going to war.

Inscriptions give some idea of the duties and responsibilities of the kings. In one inscription, King Rajendravarman reminds future kings that they have a sacred duty to protect the earth because they have conquered it.

Carved in a hallway of the temple of Angkor Wat is a magnificent scene that pictures the army of Surya-varman II going to war. It is like a parade, with columns of soldiers marching along carrying lances or bows and arrows. Leaders ride brightly painted elephants. Next comes the band, with trumpets blaring and drums beating. Clowns follow, then a somber group of Hindu religious men. A royal guard marches before the king, who is standing upright on his elephant. He looks back over the troops that follow him. Nothing, however, is known about how the Khmer fought battles, except for a scene at Angkor Wat that shows hand-to-hand fighting.

Inscriptions give the names of some of the kings' wives. Each king had many wives, but only the first wife shared her husband's successes and glory. A woman named Indradevi wrote about some of the things her sister Jayarajadevi had to do to help her husband, the king. She endured strict punishments while the king was away at war, in the hope that the gods would be pleased with her sacrifice and bring victories for the Khmer army. Indradevi does not detail the punishments, but says that her sister passed "through the fire of torments and the sea of sorrows." The king came back victorious, but soon after he returned, his wife "entered nirvana" (died).

Lives of the Monks. Inscriptions on stone slabs found in the temples give us some idea about how these religious men lived. King Yasovarman I built a temple to the Hindu god *Vishnu,* one of the gods that was worshiped by the Khmer people. He wrote that he expected the monks who lived in the temple to be only interested in pursuing good conduct and study and to be satisfied with one meal a day. He limited their possessions to "three toothpicks, a portion of husked rice, forty leaves of betel and six arec nuts, and a bundle of firewood."

Monks were expected to perform religious ceremonies. For instance, when a new statue of a god was delivered to the temple, the monks would sprinkle the statue with water and perform the "opening of the eyes" ceremony by engraving pupils on the eyes. This would assure that the god lived in the statue.

The monks' way of life and the ceremonies they performed were meant to please the gods in return for the gods' protection of the city of Angkor and the civilization of the Khmer people.

Angkor Today

After a long decline, perhaps because of sickness or because of fighting for the throne among royal family members, Angkor was captured by an army from Thailand in 1431. The Khmers abandoned Angkor and moved their capital to Phnom Penh.

Where a thriving city once stood and where thousands of people went about their daily lives, now only two Buddhist monasteries exist inside the gates of Angkor Wat.

Throughout the centuries, pilgrims have continued coming to worship at Angkor Wat. Today, tourists also come to glimpse the remains of a glorious civilization. They enjoy walking the stones of the long main entrance to the temple, which seems like a pathway to the gods, and they come to watch the sun rise over the shrines soaring skyward.

Name _____

Date _____

Using Sanskrit Numbers

From the end of the ninth century to the middle of the thirteenth century, the Khmer people built great stone temples and a capital city called Angkor in what is now Cambodia.

Highly skilled Khmer craftsmen carved religious stories and scenes of everyday life into the walls of the temples. They also carved inscriptions (writing) on freestanding slabs of stone called stelae and around the stone frames of doors. The writing was in the Khmer language and also in the Sanskrit language, which originally came from India.

Sanskrit is a parent language of most European languages, including English, French, German, and Spanish. The numerals that we call "Arabic" numerals actually came from the Sanskrit language of India. Arab scholars discovered these numerals and the number system behind them. Eventually, the numerals made their way to Europe and into European languages.

Sanskrit is no longer used today as the daily language of the Indian people. It is only used by Hindu priests and scholars.

♦ *Objective:* To recognize similarities between English and Sanskrit

♦ *Time to Complete Activity:* $\frac{1}{2}$ hour

♦ *Materials Needed:* This page, pencil

Sanskrit Numerals   **Arabic Numerals**

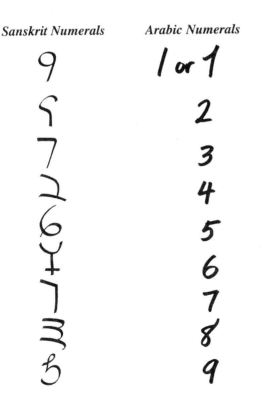

| Directions: |

_____ Draw lines, matching Sanskrit numerals to Arabic numerals.

Variation: *Our place value notation system comes from India, too (units, ones, tens, hundreds, thousands, etc., including zero). Write a number using Sanskrit numerals.*

Making a Khmer Stone Design

From the end of the ninth century to the middle of the thirteenth century, the Khmer people built great stone temples and a capital city called Angkor in what is now Cambodia.

Highly skilled Khmer craftsmen carved religious stories and scenes of everyday life into the walls of the temples. They also carved intricate designs into stone around columns, on walls, and around doors and windows.

- ◆ *Objective:* To become familiar with Khmer designs
- ◆ *Time to Complete Activity:* 1–2 hours
- ◆ *Materials Needed:* Tracing paper, large sheets of white paper, tape, pencil, overhead projector

---

Directions:

_____ Trace the designs on this page onto two separate sheets of tracing paper.

_____ Tape the tracing paper to the glass of an overhead projector and project each enlarged design onto a sheet of paper taped to a wall.

_____ Redraw each projected design on the paper taped to the wall.

_____ Photocopy the enlarged designs as many times as you like.

_____ Cut out the designs and tape them around the door of your classroom.

Variation: *These designs could be used on a book cover, newsletter, banner, etc.*

A delicate design carved into sandstone.

This grinning monster, carved in stone, is from a story that tells how the monster is commanded by the gods to eat his own body. He is still being carved on Buddhist temples in Cambodia today.

Name _____

Date _____

Using Cubits

From the end of the ninth century to the middle of the thirteenth century, the Khmer people built great stone temples and a capital city called Angkor in what is now Cambodia.

In building their temples the Khmer used the *cubit,* a unit of measurement that came from India.

A cubit is the distance from a person's elbow to the tip of his or her outstretched hand. Another unit of measurement the Khmer used was the *phyeam,* which is equal to four cubits. The temple builders at Angkor did not use a standard cubit. They probably used the king's cubit to build his temples.

♦ *Objective:* To use the cubit for measuring

♦ *Time to Complete Activity:* 1 hour

♦ *Materials Needed:* This paper, meterstick or tape measure, peel-off dots, pencil

Directions:

_____ Cubits used at Angkor ranged from .4 to .5 meters in length. With the meterstick, help each other measure your own personal cubit and place dots on the stick showing the length of each of your cubits. Write your initials in the dots.

_____ Record the length of each cubit (in meters) on the lines below. Also note whether your cubits are within the range of the ones used at Angkor.

Student (1) _____

Student (2) _____

_____ Write the lengths of your phyeams (based on your cubits) below.

Student (1) _____

Student (2) _____

_____ Help each other measure several objects around the room with your meterstick (which is now your "cubit stick") and record the measurements below. Also, measure some distances, such as length of a hallway, height of a wall, etc. Decide whether it is more appropriate to express the results in cubits or phyeams.

Object: _____

Object: _____

Object: _____

Object: _____

Variation: *Read about other civilizations that used the cubit as a unit of measurement. Is the English system of measurement used in the United States based on lengths of parts of the body? What about the metric system?*

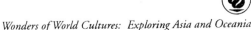

Name _____

Date _____

Thought/Discussion Questions

1. After reading the chapter, can you guess which country had a large influence on the writing and religion of the Khmer civilization?

_____

_____

_____

_____

_____

2. The Khmer built temples and carved religious scenes on temple walls in order to please the gods and gain the gods' protection for their city and people. Can you describe some ways that your family, your community, or your church seeks religious or spiritual protection?

_____

_____

_____

_____

_____

3. No one knows for sure why the Khmer craftsmen carved scenes of everyday life, like the marketplace, as well as the religious stories of the gods. What is your opinion about why they did this?

_____

_____

_____

_____

_____

CHAPTER 6: Wayang Kulit— Cultural Wonder of Java

Chapter Summary

What is the "wonder" in this story?

- Shadow theater, the *wayang kulit,* a cultural treasure of Java, Indonesia, is also one of the oldest continuous storytelling traditions in the world.

What are the major themes covered in the story and activities in this chapter?

- The wayang kulit reflects many Javanese personal and religious beliefs.
- The wayang kulit provides continuity from generation to generation in Javanese culture.

Answers to "Think About It" Questions

(page 60)

Answers will vary, but in general the Pendawa brothers with their strong character and high morals have the most *alus.* They went into exile humbly and quietly after they lost the game of dice.

The Kurawa brothers, however, are strongly *kasar*—always conniving, jealous, and downright mean.

Answers to "Thought/Discussion Questions"

(page 65) 1–2. Answers will vary.

Bibliography

Adult books

Java. Boston: APA Publications, 1993.

Lindsay, Jennifer. *Javanese Gamelan.* Oxford: Oxford, 1979.

Reiniger, Lotte. *Shadow Puppets, Shadow Theatres, and Shadow Films.* Boston: Plays, Inc., 1975.

Richter, Anne. *Arts and Crafts of Indonesia.* San Francisco: Chronicle Books, 1994.

Sorrell, Neil. *A Guide to the Gamelan.* London: Faber and Faber, 1990.

Van Ness, Edward C., and Shita Prawirohardjo. *Javanese Wayang Kulit: An Introduction.* Oxford: Oxford, 1980.

Juvenile books

Jacobs, Judy. *Indonesia, a Nation of Islands.* Minneapolis: Dillon Press, 1990.

Lynch-Watson, Janet. *The Shadow Puppet Book.* London: Sterling, 1980.

McNair, Sylvia. *Indonesia.* Chicago: Children's Press, 1993.

Poole, Frederick. *Indonesia.* New York: Franklin Watts, 1971.

Smith, Datus. *The Land and People of Indonesia.* Philadelphia: Lippincott, 1983.

CHAPTER 6:
Wayang Kulit— Cultural Wonder of Java

Javanese wayang kulit shadow puppet

ASIA

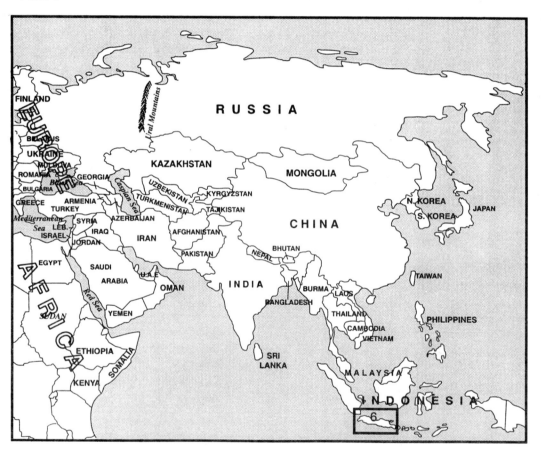

 The focus of this chapter is wayang kulit, the shadow puppetry of Java, Indonesia, performed continuously from about 800 to the present.

         Wonders of World Cultures: Exploring Asia and Oceania

Wayang Kulit

In the Indonesian language, *wayang* means "shadow" and *kulit* means "leather." *Wayang kulit* is shadow puppetry—one of the oldest continuous storytelling traditions in the world. It is a cultural treasure of the people of Java, second largest of the more than 13,000 islands that make up Indonesia.

The person who performs the wayang kulit is called the *dalang*. He sits behind a white screen that has a bright light shining on it from behind and operates puppets cut out of leather. The puppets have very intricate designs carved into them so the light can partially shine through. Sticks are attached to the hands of the puppets for moving their arms.

The dalang tells stories of gods and men based on tales that came from India about 1,300 years ago. He has a basic outline of the story that he then fills in with details from his own imagination. His performance can last as long as nine hours!

The *gamelan* orchestra sits on the same side of the screen as the puppeteer and provides music during the entire performance. This music helps create the right mood for each part of the story, and each puppet has its own "theme song" played as it enters or leaves the stage. Loud clanging marks the fight scenes.

The audience sits on the opposite side of the screen and sees the shadows of the puppets.

History of Wayang Kulit

This art form may have started around 800 and was very popular with the Javanese from the 1100's onward. During the Middle Ages, the king and nobles supported wayang kulit. It has had an impact on theater productions in other Asian countries, primarily Thailand and Malaysia, but the form that is performed in Java is still the most highly developed and refined. To this day it is a very important part of Javanese life.

Shadows of Men, Gods, and Monsters

The Javanese people are not just entertained by the wayang kulit. They totally identify with the stories and characters and love to see puppets who show beloved or hated personal qualities. They even name children after characters that have admirable qualities. If someone says, "He is like Arjuna," everyone in Javanese society would know that the man has some of the qualities of the character Arjuna, who has a strong sense of duty and morality, but is also a ladies' man.

The Javanese believe that the lives of men and gods are caught up together. The wayang kulit with its men, women, gods, and monsters, reflects these beliefs. For instance, Rama, the main character of the Ramayana story, is a human, but he was sent to earth by the gods to defeat a monster.

The Javanese also believe that the world is directed by good and bad forces. They perform rituals to try to keep these forces in balance. Certain stories that the dalang acts out are rituals in which the spirits of ancestors (good forces) are called upon to protect a rice crop or to protect a child who was born under a bad astrological sign (bad forces).

With so much riding on the wayang kulit, it's no wonder that the Javanese people are so entranced by it.

Wayang kulit puppets

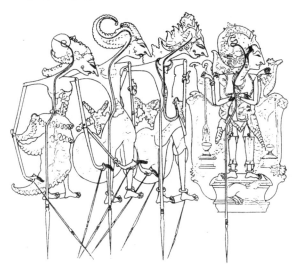

This drawing and illustrations on p. 60 from: Antiquarian, Architectural, and Landscape Illustrations of the History of Java, by Thomas Stamford Raffles. (London: Henry G. Bohn, 1844)

The Epics of Wayang Kulit

An epic is a story with heroes and sometimes villains. The dalang uses epics that came from India about 1300 years ago and fills them out with details and side stories that make them totally Javanese.

Mahabharata. The characters of this epic show the human qualities of *alus* and *kasar,* which are very important to the Javanese people.

Alus refers to a kind of personality that is considered ideal, and sometimes heroic. A person with *alus* is polite, humble, and never says mean things about others.

The opposite of *alus* is *kasar,* a kind of personality that the Javanese hate. A person with *kasar* is impolite, boastful, and mean to other people.

Here is the basic outline of the Mahabharata. (You may want to draw a genealogy chart or another visual aid as you read, to keep all the characters straight in your mind.)

◆ ◆ ◆ ◆ ◆

There was a king named Abiyasa who was old, and in his final years he just wanted to retreat to a life of meditation in the forest. He decided to choose who would follow him as the ruler of the kingdom of Ngastina. Abiyasa chose his second son, Pandu, because his first son, Drestarastra was born blind, and his third son, Widura, was crippled.

Unfortunately, soon after Pandu assumed the throne, he died. The kingship went to his five children, who were called the Pendawa. They were too young to rule, so Abiyasa's blind first son, Drestarastra, became king until the Pendawa were older.

Because the Pendawa showed qualities of leadership, their uncle Drestarastra treated them the same as his own children, who were called the Kurawa. He tried to teach the two groups of cousins to love and respect each other. They were tutored by wise teachers to become warriors of courage and high morals.

Because of the child's leadership abilities, Drestarastra chose Yudistira, the oldest of the five Pendawa, to be the next king. Drestarastra's own children were not happy about this. Duryudana, his oldest son, was persuaded by an advisor and uncle, Sangkuni, to talk Drestarastra into sending all the Pendawa to live in the jungle. Duryudana became king of Ngastina.

The Pendawa did not complain about their exile, but the Kurawa were constantly fearful that they would come back someday and claim the throne. The Kurawa wanted to get rid of the Pendawa permanently. They invited them to a banquet, and while they slept, the Kurawa set fire to their cousins' beds. The Pendawa escaped through an underground tunnel. The fire killed six innocent guests, who the Kurawa thought were the Pendawa brothers and their mother.

The Pendawa escaped to the jungle. They lived through many trials and dangers but also gained new friends and guardians, including an advisor named Kresna and the warrior Bima.

The Pendawa traveled to the kingdom of Pancala where they entered an archery contest to try to win the hand of the princess Drupadi. The brother Arjuna won the contest, and the princess became the queen of the five Pendawa.

The Kurawa discovered that the Pendawa were still alive and decided to fight them. The crippled uncle Widura and several others advised against this. They proposed that the kingdom of Ngastina be divided in half—one half for the Kurawa brothers and one half for the Pendawa brothers. Their father, the blind king Drestarastra agreed. Duryudana and his brothers also agreed and, naturally, chose the best part of the kingdom.

The Pendawa were left with land that was covered with a thick forest. After working hard, the brothers cleared the forest and turned it into a fabulous kingdom, called Ngamarta. The oldest Pendawa, Yudistira, became the king of Ngamarta.

Never content for long, the Kurawa became envious of the Pendawas' kingdom and their beautiful queen, Drupadi. They invited Yudistira to their palace to play a game of dice. He began to lose badly and finally was forced to bet Queen Drupadi. He lost her, too, and the Kurawa put her on display as a prize. Queen Drupadi swore she would wash her hair with the blood of the Kurawa brothers. The Pendawa's friend, the warrior Bima, vowed to tear them apart on the battlefield.

King Duryudana and the other Kurawa brothers invited the Pendawa to another game of dice. The Pendawa decided to play, hoping to reclaim the queen. If they lost again, they agreed to go into exile for 12 years. In the year after the exile they would have to wear disguises. If they were recognized during this time, they would have to live in exile another 12 years. Guess what! They lost again.

During their 12 years in exile, the Pendawa faced many new tests. It was also a time of great spiritual growth. Arjuna went on a famous journey to meditate on top of Mount Indrakila.

In the thirteenth year of their exile, the Pendawa put on disguises. They served in the kingdom of Wirata, whose king was a close friend, but even he did not recognize them. They even fought the Kurawa who attacked Wirata, but still no one recognized them.

At the end of the thirteenth year, the Pendawa assumed that they could return to their kingdom, but the Kurawa did not live up to the agreement and would not allow them to come back. Finally the Great War erupted and cousins fought cousins.

As warriors, the cousins had been taught to fight, but they found it difficult to kill their own relatives. At the end of the war, when all of the Kurawa brothers and most of the Pendawa brothers were dead, Duryudana's son Aswatama secretly entered the Pendawa camp and murdered all the women and children. The only child who survived was an unborn baby who was taken from its mother's womb and revived by the Pendawa friend and advisor, Kresna. This child became the ancestor of the kings of Java.

A Javanese Story

In a typical wayang kulit performance, the dalang takes part of the Mahabharata and weaves a new story from it.

The story is set during the time that the two sets of cousins, the Pendawa and the Kurawa, were living in the two separate kingdoms that had been created from one kingdom.

From his imagination the dalang creates a princess, Dewi Rukmini. She wants to find a husband, but she requires him to answer a question to her satisfaction before she will marry him. Her question is: "What is the real meaning behind the words male and female?"

Male characters that the audience is familiar with, such as Arjuna, the ladies' man of the Pendawa brothers, are all interested in the princess's offer.

From all corners of the land, the suitors set out for the kingdom of Kumbina, where the princess lives. Battles are fought along the way because many of the suitors are already enemies. The gamelan orchestra plays special clanging music with marching and battle scenes.

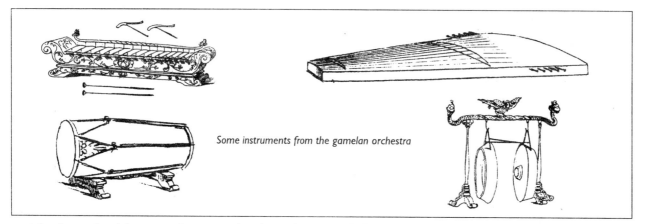

Some instruments from the gamelan orchestra

At times, the dalang uses humor to break up the story. Clowns try to offer advice to Arjuna, but they wind up fighting among themselves and challenge each other to a singing contest.

When all the suitors have arrived in Kumbina, there is much chasing, bumbling, magic, mistaken identity, and wrong answers to the princess's question. Finally, the one who wins the hand of the princess answers this way: "That which is male is contained in the seed of a first-class man, and that which is female is contained in the womb of a first-class woman."

This is just a bare outline of the story. The performance goes on for hours. The dalang uses all of his skill and what he learned from his father, who learned the craft from his father, to enthrall the audience. Children sit as close to the dalang as possible, using paper puppets to imitate the action of the play. In the process they learn the stories and characters of wayang kulit and their Javanese history, just as their parents learned it before them.

Think About It—

Which characters in the Mahabharata show the most alus? Which show the most kasar?

Making Your Own Shadow Puppets

In the Indonesian language *wayang* means "shadow" and *kulit* means "leather." *Wayang kulit* is shadow puppetry—one of the oldest continuous storytelling traditions in the world. It is a cultural treasure of the people of Java, second largest of the more than 13,000 islands that make up Indonesia.

The person who performs the wayang kulit is the *dalang*. He sits behind a white screen with a bright light shining on it from behind and operates puppets cut out of leather. Sticks are attached to the hands of the puppets for moving their arms. The *gamelan* orchestra sits on the same side of the screen as the puppeteer and provides music during the entire performance, which can last up to nine hours!

Many of these stories are epics full of heroes and villains. These stories originally came from India.

◆ **Objective:** To create your own shadow puppet theater

◆ **Time to Complete Activity:** 4–5 hours

◆ **Materials Needed:** Straws; poster board; scissors; masking tape; hole punch; paper fasteners; large piece of cardboard (about 36 by 20 inches); craft knife; large sheet of white paper; table lamp; percussion instruments, such as drum, gong, xylophone, and bells; research materials on epics

---

Directions:

_____ Decide on an epic you would like to perform. Choose one scene from the epic. Some suggestions are *Beowulf*, the *Odyssey*, the *Iliad*, and *Paradise Lost*. (Or, you can choose a folktale, such as the story of the hero Paul Bunyan.)

_____ Cut out the characters from the poster board. If you want the characters to have movable parts, you will need to cut out the individual parts. For instance, a monster's arm could move up and down if you cut out the monster and one separate arm piece. Just one movable piece per puppet may be enough for now.

_____ Punch a hole in the part that will move and a hole in the body where the part will be attached. Line up both holes and join them with a paper fastener.

_____ Tape a straw (your handle) to the back of the body. Tape another to the back of the part that moves.

_____ Create scenery with cutouts of trees, houses, and whatever else you need taped to straws.

_____ To make the wayang kulit stage, set up the piece of cardboard on a tabletop and fold back the sides about 10 inches so that the stage can stand on its own. (See drawing next page.)

_____ With the craft knife, cut out a square about 12 × 12 inches in the center panel of the cardboard stage. Place the white paper on the dalang's side of the square and tape the edges with masking tape.

_____ Place the lamp behind the stage to shine on the center panel.

_____ After practicing, you're ready to perform your shadow puppetry. Members of the group can use the percussion instruments to create sound effects and music to go with the performance.

(continued)

Making Your Own Shadow Puppets (continued)

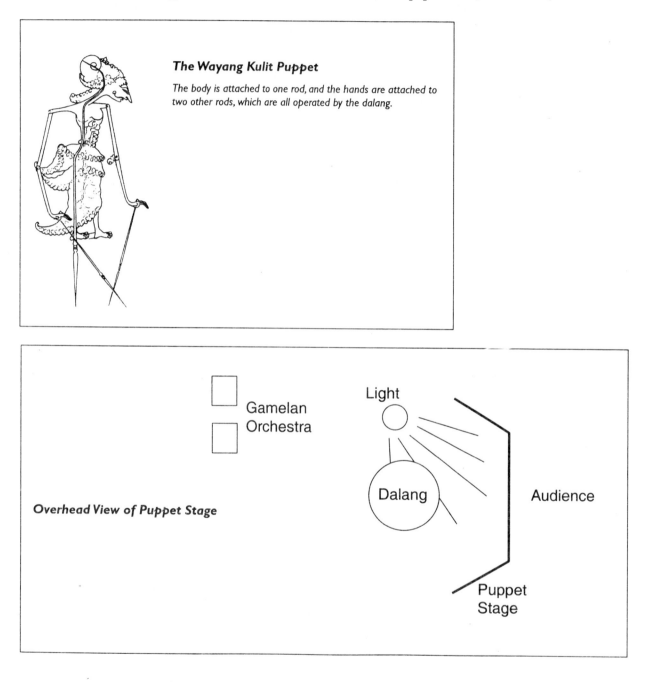

The Wayang Kulit Puppet

The body is attached to one rod, and the hands are attached to two other rods, which are all operated by the dalang.

Gamelan Orchestra

Overhead View of Puppet Stage

Light

Dalang

Audience

Puppet Stage

Name _____

Date _____

The Ramayana

Wayang kulit, the shadow puppetry of Java, is one of the oldest continuous storytelling traditions in the world. It is a cultural treasure of the people of Java, second largest of the more than 13,000 islands that make up Indonesia.

The person who performs the wayang kulit is called the *dalang.* Many of the stories performed by the dalang are epics full of heroes and villains. One of these is the *Ramayana,* which came from India about 1,300 years ago.

◆ *Objective:* To create dialogue for the Ramayana

◆ *Time to Complete Activity:* 1 hour

◆ *Materials Needed:* Paper, pencil

Directions:

_____ Read the basic outline of the Ramayana on these pages.

_____ Rewrite the story, making it more interesting by inventing dialogue and providing details. Use your imagination! (See paragraph 3 in the story below for suggestions.)

The Ramayana

Rama was born to King Dasarata and Queen Raguwati. Before Rama was born, the gods had decided that he would be a hero and would have to face many tests. He was the human form of the god Wisnu, a monster who had been bothering the kingdom for many years.

King Dasarata had two other wives. One was Dewi Sumitra, who gave birth to a son named Leksmana. The other wife was Dewi Kekayi, who had a son named Barata.

The three half brothers, Rama, Leksmana, and Barata, were raised together. Their teacher was a wise man named Wiswamitra, who taught them how to behave as warriors belonging to the high level of Indonesian society. (*Suggestion:* Write about a time when Wiswamitra was training the boys. What skills would he teach them? What would he say to them?)

When the three brothers were young men, they traveled throughout their own and neighboring kingdoms, and Rama found a young woman he wanted to marry, the beautiful Dewi Sinta. Her father held a contest to choose the young man she would marry. Whoever could string her father's huge bow could have Dewi Sinta's hand in marriage. Rama succeeded at this task.

When the three brothers returned home, their father decided it was time to appoint the son who would succeed him as king when he died. He wanted to appoint Rama, but one of the three wives, Dewi Kekayi, reminded him of a promise he had made to her years ago. She had nursed him back to health after he was wounded in battle, and he had promised her then that their son Barata would become king when the time came. Because he was bound by his promise, the king had to allow Barata to assume the throne, and he was forced to send Rama, Dewi Sinta, and Leksmana to live in the jungle for 14 years. Because of his strong character, Rama left without any feelings of anger.

The three exiles settled down in the jungle and built a small house. After a while, the female monster Sarapenaka, sister of the monster King Dasamuka, starting bothering them, and Leksmana drove her away by cutting off her ear.

(continued)

The Ramayana (continued)

Sarapenaka complained to her brother Dasamuka, who sent another female monster named Marica to get revenge. Marica took the form of a golden deer. Rama ran after the deer to try to catch it because Dewi Sinta said she would like to have it as a pet. When they were deep in the jungle, Marica resumed her real form and cried out. Leksmana heard the cries and thought that Rama was in danger. He ran into the jungle to save Rama, leaving Dewi Sinta alone. King Dasamuka took this opportunity to kidnap Dewi Sinta, taking her away in his flying chariot.

Rama and Leksmana heard of the kidnapping from the great Garuda bird who tried to save Dewi Sinta. Unfortunately, he was fatally wounded, but was able to tell of the kidnapping before he died.

Rama and Leksmana set out to find Dewi Sinta. In their travels they came upon a great kingdom of monkeys. After they helped the monkey king Sugriwa defeat his brother, they gained a loyal friend and his entire army, including the warrior monkey Anoman.

Anoman, the warrior monkey, was sent to King Dasamuka's kingdom, where Dewi Sinta was being held. Anoman, who was really the adopted son of the God of the Wind, crossed the ocean in one great leap to reach the monster's kingdom. There he found Dewi Sinta and showed her a ring that came from Rama. This convinced her that Rama had sent the monkey to help her. Unfortunately, Dasamuka's son, Megananda, captured the monkey warrior, but Anoman escaped just as Dasamuka set fire to his tail in an attempt to burn him alive. Before he left, Anoman set fire to most of Dasamuka's kingdom.

With the army of monkeys, Rama, Leksmana, and Anoman attacked what was left of Dasamuka's kingdom to try to save Dewi Sinta. To get across the ocean that separated the kingdoms of Dasamuka and Rama, the monkey army built a huge bridge. One of Dasamuka's brothers was killed in a horrible battle. In the end Anoman killed Dasamuka by bludgeoning him with the top of a nearby mountain, which he had torn off with his godlike strength.

Rama, Dewi Sinta, and Leksmana returned to their own kingdom and ruled for many years in peace.

(Adapted from *Javanese Wayland Kulit: An Introduction,* by Edward C. Van Ness and Shita Prawirohardjo, Kuala Lumpur: Oxford University Press, 1980.)

Thought/Discussion Questions

1. Do you think the personal qualities of *alus* and *kasar* are very important in your own culture? Why or why not?

_____

_____

_____

_____

_____

_____

2. In addition to what you read in the chapter, how do you think Javanese culture benefits from the wayang kulit? Does your culture have forms of entertainment that provide similar benefits to the people in your own community?

_____

_____

_____

_____

_____

_____

CHAPTER 7: **Cultural Wonders of the Samurai**

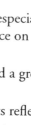

Chapter Summary

What are the "wonders" in this story?

- Classic features of Japanese culture, such as the Noh theater, that developed during the time when the samurai were in power.

What are the major themes covered in the story and activities in this chapter?

- The arts play a large part in Japanese culture.

- The religions of Japan, especially Zen Buddhism, had a profound influence on society and arts in Japan.
- Contact with China had a great impact on the Japanese.
- Japanese society and arts reflect a basic love of nature and natural beauty.

Answers to "Think About It" Question

(page 72)

The tea ceremony is still practiced in Japan and so is landscape gardening. Traditional sword making is practiced by only a few men who are considered "national living treasures" of Japan. Of the more than 3,000 Noh plays that were written during the Middle Ages, only about 230 still survive and are performed, some only once a decade.

Answers to "Thought/Discussion Questions"

(page 76) 1–3. Answers will vary.

Bibliography

Adult books

Bownas, Geoffrey, and Anthony Thwaite, trans. *The Penguin Book of Japanese Verse*. Baltimore: Penguin, 1964.

Cook, Harry. *Samurai: The Story of a Warrior Tradition*. New York: Sterling, 1993.

Hammitzsch, Horst. *Zen in the Art of the Tea Ceremony*. New York: St. Martin's, 1980.

Komparu, Kunio. *The Noh Theater: Principles and Perspectives*. New York: Weatherhill/Tankosha, 1983.

Kuck, Loraine E. *The Art of Japanese Gardens*. New York: John Day, 1940.

Quinn, Lee Early. *The Easy Magic of Japanese Flower Arrangement*. Rutland, Vermont: Tuttle, 1965.

Rexroth, Kenneth. *The Burning Heart: The Women Poets of Japan*. New York: Seabury, 1977.

Sato, Hiroaki. *Legends of the Samurai*. Woodstock, NY: Overlook Press, 1995.

Storry, Richard. *The Way of the Samurai*. New York: Putnam, 1978.

Till, Barry. *Samurai: The Cultured Warrior.* Victoria, British Columbia: Sono Nis Press, 1984.

Turnbull, Stephen. *Samurai Warfare.* London: Arms and Armour Press, 1996.

Juvenile books

MacDonald, Fiona. *A Samurai Castle.* New York: P. Bedrick Books, 1995.

Roberts, Jenny. *History Highlights: Samurai Warriors.* London: Gloucester Press, 1990.

Steel, Anne. *How They Lived: A Samurai Warrior.* Vero Beach, Florida: Rourke Enterprises, Inc., 1988.

CHAPTER 7:
Cultural Wonders of the Samurai

The art of flower arranging, called ikebana, is an important part of Japanese life. It became a form of art in the fourteenth to fifteenth centuries.

This illustration and most others in this chapter from Japan: Its History and Literature, by Captain F. Brinkley (Boston & Tokyo: J.B. Millet Co., 1901)

ASIA

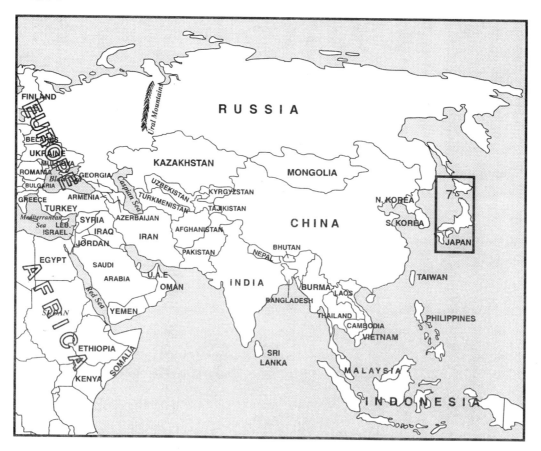

 The focus of this chapter is the warrior class of Japanese society—the samurai—who controlled Japan from 1185 to 1868.

       Wonders of World Cultures: Exploring Asia and Oceania

JAPAN

Samurai Means "One Who Serves"

In tenth-century Japan brave warriors, skilled in the use of bow, spear, and sword, served as protectors for nobles and their families who lived in rural outlying areas far from the capital, Kyoto. These warriors also helped the noble masters take over lands from other families.

The warriors and their masters in the rural provinces became known as *samurai*—a new class of people in Japanese society. They got stronger and stronger, and sometimes they rebelled against the emperor and his government in Kyoto. One group, known as the Taira, rebelled against Kyoto in the tenth century.

Because the emperor and the city nobles were not fighters, they started using some of the samurai warriors as police and guards in the capital. One of these samurai groups, the Minamoto, helped defeat the Taira rebellion.

Later, in 1156, the two samurai groups fought each other again. The Taira gained control and began to take power from the central government. There was still an emperor and his court, but they had no power. The idea of serving a master was so strong in the samurai leaders, however, that they still thought of themselves as servants of the emperor even though the samurai held the power. Between 1180 and 1185, the two main samurai groups fought an epic struggle called the Gempei War. This war is the source for many of the stories and people in Japanese legends and theater. It started with the rebellion of an aged Minamoto veteran and ended with complete defeat of the Taira forces.

One folktale says that the ghosts of defeated Taira warriors linger on the seashore where the last fatal battle took place. Crabs in the area have markings that look like samurai war helmets. These are the souls of dead Taira warriors, according to the tale.

The samurai winners of the war ruled Japan from 1185 to 1868. Samurai rule emphasized the warrior might and strict discipline. They were always ready to kill or be killed. Through their bravery and fierce fighting they successfully defeated two Mongol invasions in the late 1200's.

The samurai class also started enjoying some of the cultural pursuits of the emperor and his court. In the 1300's, many well-known features of classic Japanese culture evolved from older traditions, including the Noh theater, the tea ceremony, gardening, and the art of making swords.

To understand the arts of Japan, it is helpful to learn about the religions of Japan.

Religions of Japan

Shinto is a religion that started in Japan. It centers on worship of nature. The people had a deep respect for mountains, streams, trees, and the soil. They also worshiped the sun in the form of a sun goddess, and they believed that the first emperor was

Wonders of World Cultures: Exploring Asia and Oceania

an ancestor of the sun goddess. They also believed in many lesser but still important gods.

Another religion of the Japanese people is Buddhism, which originally came from India and reached Japan in the sixth century A.D.

Zen Buddhism is a type of Buddhism that came to be widely accepted in Japan in the 1100's. Zen Buddhism helped the samurai because it stressed action and instinct rather than thought, feeling, and questioning. Also, Zen taught that there is no difference between life and death. Neither is worthy of consideration.

Through meditation, a samurai could achieve the Zen spirit and the willpower to force all thought and questioning from his mind so he could fight and die without hesitation in the service of his master and country. Death to him must be "lighter than a feather."

Both Zen and Shinto stress a natural, simple way of looking at the world, which appealed to the samurai. He had to be able to throw off the many distractions around him and focus on the single purpose of his life—being a warrior who was ready to die.

The Tea Ceremony

Zen monks brought this art form from China to Japan. It provided a way for samurai warriors to relax, if only temporarily.

Leaving his sword outside, the samurai entered the tea hut through a low sliding door. Then the rituals of the tea ceremony would begin.

The samurai first knelt and bowed deeply to the floor. The only decorations in the tea house were a scroll of calligraphy (fine handwriting) and a carefully arranged vase of flowers, which the samurai and other guests at the tea ceremony quietly contemplated. Mats of rice-straw covered the floor. A heavy iron kettle stood on a wooden support over a bed of hot coals. Tea utensils, bowls and bamboo tea whisks, were set out on a table. With other guests, the samurai sat motionless and watched silently as the tea

preparer boiled the water and prepared the tea. The motions of the tea server followed a slow and graceful ritual. The Samurai drank the tea in three sips, the last sip being a loud "slurp." He and other guests often admired the beautiful tea utensils, and sometimes composed poetry or played the lute. In this sanctuary of tranquility, beauty, and ritual, samurai could put aside the cares of the warrior's world.

A Samurai in Full Armor

At 10 years of age a boy of the samurai class started his training. He learned fencing, archery, wrestling, horseback riding, spear throwing, and how to plan a battle. He also learned how to commit suicide, if necessary. At 15 the young samurai became an adult and could wear his hair pulled back into a ponytail in the warrior style. He could also officially carry a sword, his most prized possession.

The Art of Making Swords

Japanese craftsmen achieved a high level of skill in making objects of war, including bows and arrows and matchlock guns, after they came into contact with the Portuguese in the mid 1500's.

The armor that samurai warriors wore was made of hundreds of lacquered steel or leather scales laced together with silk braids of different colors.

The object where craftsmanship reached its highest level, however, was the sword, considered the "soul of the samurai." It represented the warrior's self-discipline, devotion to a master, and fighting skill. A samurai cleaned his sword every day, wiping the blade forty times, then reapplying oil.

Before a sword maker started to make a sword, he performed rituals. To purify his body he washed in cold water and prayed for guidance. The swordsmith tried to be clean in mind and body so no evil thoughts would enter the blade as he worked on it and later cause it to commit evil acts.

The warrior needed a sword that was strong but flexible so it would not break in battle. First, the sword maker heated pieces of iron in a charcoal fire until they were cherry red. Then, he hammered the hot iron into a thin sheet, folded it in half, reheated it, and hammered it out again. This process would be repeated up to 18 times. When the gently curved blade was finished, it was polished to a high sheen.

The sword guard (a piece between the handle and the blade) was highly decorated with landscape scenes or events from history. The sword handle was covered with the skin of the giant ray (fish), which is like ivory, and wrapped diagonally with silk braid to provide a good grip.

A finished sword had to be handled in a certain way. As it was pulled out of the cover, it was turned with the cutting edge upward, and the blade could never be touched with the hand or fingers.

Noh Theater

This form of drama grew out of early Buddhist dances. In the 1300's it became the main form of entertainment of samurai society. The Noh plays were taken from samurai stories of war and from classic Japanese tales.

All of the actors were men, who presented the story through song, dance, and wordless gestures. Every movement had symbolic meaning. Originally these plays were performed outside in very bare settings. Sometimes wealthy samurai hired actors to perform at their homes.

The actors wore elaborate and colorful silk robes and masks, which could represent a male or a female of any age. Originally there were three types of masks: gods or demons, old men, and women. To show expressions, the masks were tilted in different ways, to catch light or cast shadows.

Noh Theater

Before the actor went onstage, he would put on the mask and look through the eyeholes at his image in a mirror. In this way he tried to become the character he was playing.

Landscape Gardening

The samurai nobles and warriors certainly were not the first people in Japan to create beautiful gardens. After the Japanese made contact with China, in the early 600's, they tried to make gardens like those they had seen in China. One of the features of these gardens was an artificial island and rock formation in the middle of a pond. This was meant to re-create a scene from a Chinese fable in which a mountain rises up from the sea. People of the upper classes, who were the only ones who could afford to have gardens, would float around the pond in little boats and write poetry.

Later, in the 800's and 900's, the emperor and his court spent a lot of their time in cultural and artistic pursuits. They built splendid houses and gardens, wrote romantic poetry, played music, and created and wore beautiful bright-colored costumes. They stopped trying to copy Chinese ideas and began to develop their own style of gardens. These gardens showed every season of the year in its brightest colors. For instance, they would plant red plum, cherry, and rock azalea in one area to create the most colorful bloom in springtime.

What the world thinks of as the "classic" Japanese garden developed during the reign of the samurai and reflects the Zen influence on Japanese society. The gaiety and bright colors of the emperor's gardens gave way to the simplicity and naturalness of the Zen-inspired garden. Gardeners used stones, plants, and water to create a scene that was simple and natural. Sometimes plants and rocks were symbols for other things. For instance, a row of stones might be symbols for a group of junks (boats) anchored in a harbor. A typical plan for a garden called for three parts—a background, a middle, and a foreground. A distant mountain and natural hills might form the background; a lake and artificial hills would form the middle area; the foreground, or area closest to the viewer, might include an edge of the lake and a stretch of ground between buildings. Small fingers of land projecting into the lake and rocks placed along its edges added interest. The middle area of the garden might have rock arrangements, a small waterfall, or a stone bridge.

These beautiful natural gardens provided a place for the samurai to relax and, in the Zen tradition, a place to meditate.

Think About It—

After the samurai control of Japan faded in the 1800's, which of the cultural and religious activities described in this chapter do you think have continued to the present day?

A Tea House

A tea house, or hut, for conducting the tea ceremony was usually set in a bamboo thicket or among trees. A garden area of plants, rocks, ponds, and perhaps a bridge would be created near the house. In this natural setting, the samurai could put aside his daily cares and just enjoy the sound of the water boiling in the iron kettle and watch the tea server artfully prepare and serve tea.

Ikebana—Japanese Flower Arranging

In the 1300's, many of the well-known features of classic Japanese culture—the Noh theater, the tea ceremony, landscape gardening, and the art of making swords—evolved from older traditions. Flower arranging, or *ikebana,* also became part of Japanese culture. Starting in the 1400's, Buddhist priests used ikebana in religious worship.

Drinking tea and the tea ceremony were also brought to Japan by religious men. From the Middle Ages through today, a flower arrangement is usually the only decoration in the room or tea hut where the tea ceremony takes place. The arrangement is displayed in a special place, called an alcove, in the wall.

Many styles of ikebana evolved over the centuries, from early, formal styles to the modern abstract style. In this activity you follow the modern style known as *moribana,* in which three main plant stems are arranged in a low, open container.

- ♦ *Objective:* To learn something about ikebana

- ♦ *Time to Complete Activity:* 1–2 hours

- ♦ *Materials Needed:* Plant material (You need to gather your own plant material: see below); a *kenzan,* which is a flat device with spikes used to hold up plant stems, also sometimes called a "frog," available at flower shops or nurseries; a low, open container, like a plant tray; pebbles or marbles; sharp scissors; white poster board or other large white paper

---

Directions:

_____ Cut the top of the poster board so it has the shape of an arch.

_____ Tape the poster board to a wall over an uncluttered table. This is your "alcove."

_____ Gather your plant materials. From home or near school collect flowers and leaves *with stems.* Stems should range in size from the width of your little finger to about a quarter of the width of your little finger. All kinds of plant materials, even branches with no leaves, are usable—the more interesting, the better!

_____ Look at your plant materials. Look for interesting shapes, curves, and textures. Decide which side looks best.

_____ Choose three stems that you think will look good together. After placing the kenzan in the bottom of the container, push the ends of the stems into the kenzan to keep them in place. Keep these ideas in mind as you do this:

_____ Try to form a triangle with the tips of your three stems while looking at them from the front.

_____ Place the bottoms of your three stems close together in the kenzan.

_____ Create a center of interest, called a *negime,* that is shorter than your three main stems. For instance, you could place smaller flowers (with short stems) near the bottom of your longer stems to form a negime.

_____ Your arrangement should seem alive and growing as if the flowers or stems are "talking to one another." Relax and try something unusual!

_____ Add enough pebbles or marbles to the container to cover up kenzan and bottom of stems. Position the arrangement carefully in front of white poster board "alcove."

Variation: *After you have some experience arranging flowers and stems, use scissors to cut leaves off stems and otherwise shape your plant material.*

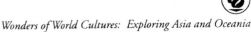

Name _____

Date _____

Writing and Performing Japanese Poetry

From the fifth century, when the Japanese borrowed Chinese characters to write their own language, the Japanese have written poetry about every aspect of their lives. Most often, they write about nature.

By the light or dark
Of the green in the fields
Where young shoots sprout,
It can clearly be seen
Where the snow thawed first.

Bringing flowers with it,
Hira's mountain squall
Swept over the lake.

A boat, rowed through,
Left flowers in its wake.

—Kunaikyo (died 1207)

(Poem translated by Geoffrey Bownas and Anthony Thwaite. *The Penguin Book of Japanese Verse.* Harmondsworth, Middlesex, Great Britain: Penguin Books Ltd., 1964.)

The five-line *tanka* poem was developed during the Heian period (794–1185), when the emperor and his court spent much of their time in cultural pursuits, such as writing poetry, painting, and playing music.

Sometimes the tanka poem is in two parts of five lines each like the one above.

♦ *Objective:* To write a five-line tanka poem
♦ *Time to Complete Activity:* Several hours, spread over one or several days
♦ *Materials Needed:* Paper, pencil, resource materials

Directions:

_____ Read as many traditional Japanese poems as you can, focusing on the five-line type. Discuss with others in your group the characteristics of Japanese poetry. Do the ends of the lines rhyme? Are there a lot of adjectives? Are the poems straightforward or subtle? Does there seem to be symbolic or underlying meaning?

_____ Each person in the group should select something in the natural world that he or she will be able to return to several times during the day. It can be a scene viewed from a distance or a something seen up close—perhaps just one flower blossom. Try to choose a setting that is free from distractions.

_____ Sitting as comfortably as possible in front of your natural scene or object, relax and close your eyes. Try to force all thoughts from your mind and concentrate on your breathing. After several minutes, open your eyes and look at your subject as if you had never seen it before. Pay attention to every detail—leaves, flowers, insects, grass, sky, wind, and whatever else you see, hear, smell, and feel. Write down the time of day and your impressions.

_____ Return to this spot several times during the day, jotting down your impressions each time.

_____ Write a five-line tanka-style poem based on your notes. Try to project a feeling of how your natural scene or object changed during the day.

_____ Take turns reading your poems to others in your group. Discuss things you liked about one another's poetry.

Variation: *Have a poetry competition! All those who wish to participate (and who have some experience composing poetry) could read their poems to the whole class, who will vote on their favorite poems.*

Noh Masks

In the 1300's, under samurai warrior lords, many of the well-known features of classic Japanese culture evolved from older traditions, including the Noh theater, the tea ceremony, landscape gardening, and the art of making swords.

In the Middle Ages, Noh theater became the main form of entertainment for the samurai class in Japanese society. Most of the stories of the Noh plays come from traditional Japanese and Asian tales and samurai legends of war.

The Tale of Genji, written by the Lady Murasaki Shikibu in the early eleventh century, is one of the classic Japanese stories that inspired the type of Noh dramas called "woman plays." The story revolves around Prince Genji and the women in his life.

Actors (all men in traditional Noh theater) wear masks. To express emotions, the actor raises, lowers, and turns his head so that his mask catches the light or casts shadows.

These masks show the range of emotions in women's masks—from quiet joy to violent rage.

♦ *Objective:* To create a display showing different kinds of Noh masks

♦ *Time to Complete Activity:* 2–3 hours

♦ *Materials Needed:* White poster board, scissors, felt-tip pens, tongue depressors, glue, mirror

---

Directions:

_____ Using the masks on this page as general guides, make a life-size mask for each type of Noh mask listed below. (Note that eyebrows are placed very high on the forehead.)

_____ Glue a tongue depressor "handle" to each mask.

_____ Place the masks and a mirror in an area of your classroom where students can hold the masks in front of their faces and look at themselves through the eyeholes. Provide a notebook in the mask area so people can jot down their impressions for others to read.

Types of Noh masks (and some qualities they project)

- Old man masks (gentle, mean, deathlike)
- Masks with strange faces (jealous or insane characters, monkeylike face with bulging eyes, flushed elflike face, demons, dragons, barking lion-dog, horns)
- Gods and Buddhas
- Young man masks (sensitive, handsome, blind, grief-stricken)
- Middle-age man masks (warrior in his fighting prime, mysterious ghosts)
- Young woman masks (gentle, beautiful, elegant)
- Middle-age woman masks (slightly older, sadder)
- Old woman masks (ghosts, crazy, beautiful, mystical spirit woman, woman in death)

Variation: *Study Noh theater and present a Noh play to your class. The drama class or club in your school may be willing and able to help.*

Name _____

Date _____

Thought/Discussion Questions

1. To your way of thinking how is the Japanese tea ceremony an "art form"?

_____

_____

_____

_____

_____

_____

2. Some of the cultural pursuits, like the tea ceremony, that you read about in the chapter originally came from religious worship. Can you think of any artistic or cultural activities in our society that came from religious worship?

_____

_____

_____

_____

_____

_____

3. Do you think there are any remnants of the samurai class in modern Japanese society?

_____

_____

_____

_____

_____

_____

CHAPTER 8: The Taj Mahal— Wonder of India

Chapter Summary

What is the "wonder" in this story?

- The Taj Mahal, which is considered by some to be one of the most beautiful buildings in the world.

What are the major themes covered in the story and activities in this chapter?

- Muslim rulers, called Moguls or Mughals, whose rule over large areas of India started in the Middle Ages, brought a mix of styles and influences to India, including Persian designs that used symmetry and repeating patterns.

- One of these rulers, Shah Jahan, built a tomb in memory of his wife. This complex, which blends Mogul and Persian elements, is considered by many to be one of the most beautiful buildings in the world.

- A strain of romanticism underlies the Taj Mahal, especially in the legends surrounding the relationship of Shah Jahan and his wife, Mumtaz Mahal, and the motivation behind the building of the Taj.

Answers to "Think About It" Question

(page 82)

The story hints at some of the possible reasons why there are no portraits of Mumtaz Mahal. High-born women such as Mumtaz Mahal did not show their faces to people of lower classes, which included portrait painters. Also, in general, women were required by Muslim law to hide their faces behind a veil.

Answers to "Discovering the Underlying Grid of the Taj Mahal" _____

(page 84)

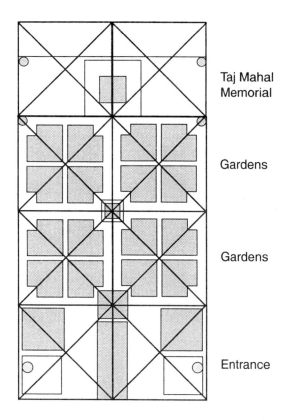

Taj Mahal
Memorial

Gardens

Gardens

Entrance

Answers to "Thought/Discussion Questions" _____

(page 86)

1. Answers will vary.

2. Answers will vary.

Bibliography _____

Adult books

Begley, W. E., and Z. A. Desai, compilers and translators. *Taj Mahal, the Illumined Tomb: An Anthology of Seventeenth-Century Mughal and European Documentary Sources.* Seattle: University of Washington Press, 1989.

Carroll, David. *The Taj Mahal.* New York: Newsweek, 1972.

Nou, Jean-Louis. *Taj Mahal.* New York: Abbeville Press, 1993.

Pratapaditya, Pal, Janice Leoshko, Joseph M. Dye, III, and Stephen Markel. *Romance of the Taj Mahal.* Thames and Hudson, 1989.

Rai, Raghu. *Taj Mahal.* New York: Vendome Press, 1987.

Magazine articles

Bond, Constance. "The Man Who Built the Taj." *Smithsonian,* Vol. 28 (August 1997), pp. 56–61.

CHAPTER 8:
The Taj Mahal— Wonder of India

Many people think that the Taj Mahal is one of the most beautiful buildings in the world.

ASIA

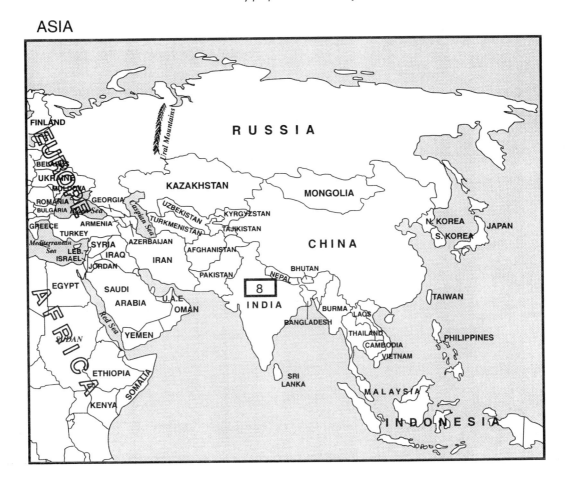

⑧   *The focus of this chapter is the Taj Mahal of India, begun in 1632.*

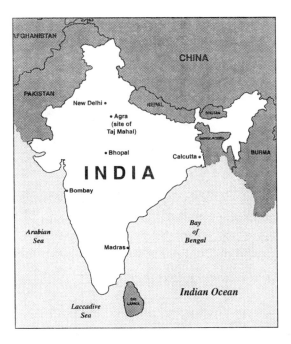

A Wonder of Dazzling White Marble

Built during a twenty-year period starting in 1632, the Taj Mahal of Agra has been called one of the architectural wonders of the world. It is a magnificent tomb, built by a Muslim ruler of India for his beloved wife, who died in childbirth.

The Taj Mahal complex is entered through the arches of a three-story gate. The gate is a building in itself, with many mysterious rooms and hallways. No one knows what these rooms were used for.

After you walk through the gate, you see a long rectangular pool of water. In the center is a square holding tank with five fountains. Along the sides of the pool are strips of grass inlaid with repeating patterns of marble and small cedar trees planted in perfectly straight lines leading up to the tomb. The pool draws your eye to the Taj Mahal itself, which looks small at first and very far away. As you walk toward the tomb you see how truly large and magnificent it is—20 stories tall! The eight-sided tomb, which is topped by one large dome and four smaller domes, sits on a large rectangular platform that has towers called minarets on the corners.

Visitors from every country have visited the Taj Mahal and described its wonders.

The writer Rudyard Kipling wrote, "The mists lay on the ground, so that the splendour [the Taj] seemed to be floating free of the earth. . . . Then as the train sped forward, and the mists shifted, and the sun shone upon the mists, the Taj took a hundred new shapes, each perfect and each beyond description."

Many visitors preferred moonlit views. In 1915 Prince William of Sweden described the Taj at night as a "lustrous Oriental pearl . . . a white jewel enclosed in a frame of dark cypresses, with the flashing starry sky as a background."

At midday, when the temperature can soar to over 100 degrees, the white marble of the Taj Mahal shines so brightly that most visitors can only look at it through half-closed eyes or very dark sunglasses.

Inside the Taj Mahal, however, the huge burial hall is very dim. The only light comes through screened windows far up on the walls. In the middle of the hall is an eight-sided marble screen that protects monuments to the ruler and his wife. Their remains are actually buried under the floor of the hall.

The coffin-shaped monuments are decorated with precious stones set in patterns, called mosaics. Beautiful repeating flower and vine patterns frame fine Arabic calligraphy that tells about the goodness of the queen, the emperor, and God.

A Love Story with a Sad Ending

Who was the man who built the Taj Mahal? And who was the woman whose untimely death caused so much grief that her husband, the emperor, built a monument that took twenty years to complete?

Shah Jahan was the fifth of a line of Muslim emperors (followers of the Islamic religion) whose rule over India was strongest from about 1556 to 1707. They are called Moguls (or Mughals) and originally came from an area north of Afghanistan.

The native Indian population followed the Hindu religion, so they were at odds with their Muslim rulers most of the time.

The Taj Mahal as seen from the entrance gate. From Things Seen in India, by T. L. Pennell. (London: Seeley, Service & Co. Ltd., 1913)

In 1592, a young prince named Khurram was born to a Hindu-princess mother and a half-Hindu father. As he grew, Khurram became a strong believer in the Muslim religion and traditions. His teachers were Muslim religious men called Sufis. They taught him science, medicine, grammar, mathematics, astronomy, and geology. He also learned Arabic, which is the language of the Koran (the holy book of Islam), and Persian, the language of the Mogul culture. The Persian Empire, centered in what is now Iran, had a strong influence over surrounding areas, including India.

When Khurram was a young prince of sixteen, so the story goes, he went to a special market where high-born girls of Muslim society, who usually had to stay at home, were allowed to be shopkeepers for a day. They could take off the veils that usually covered their faces and temporarily become haggling merchants. They also teased and flirted with the "customers"—young men who competed with each other to attract the attention of the young women.

It was here that the prince met his future wife, fifteen-year-old Arjumand Banu Begam, the daughter of the Mogul prime minister. Poets of the day wrote that she was very beautiful, but no portraits of her have survived.

When the prince came to her market stall, he was attracted to her at once. He asked how much she was asking for a large piece of glass that was cut to look like a diamond. She replied that it really was a diamond and that she didn't think he had enough money to buy it—10,000 rupees. Without saying a word he reached into his sleeve and handed her 10,000 rupees. Then he took the glass and left.

The next day the prince asked his father if he could marry the prime minister's daughter. His father agreed, but said the young prince would have to wait five years before he could marry Arjumand.

The prince was expected to marry for reasons other than love; for instance, to seal an agreement with a foreign power. For this reason and because he was allowed by Muslim law to have four wives, he first married a Persian princess.

Finally, the prince was allowed to marry Arjumand, who was renamed Mumtaz Mahal, which means "chosen one of the palace," by her father-in-law, the emperor.

According to poets and other writers of the day, Mumtaz Mahal was more lovely than the moon and stars. It was said that she cared about the poor and gave out food to beggars who called to her from outside the palace walls.

Like her husband and others of her time, however, she also enjoyed watching the torture of prisoners.

When the prince and Mumtaz Mahal had been married nineteen years, the emperor died. The prince claimed the title of emperor of India and renamed himself Shah Jahan, which means "the king of the world." He ordered his brothers and all close male relatives to be killed so that there would be no one left to challenge his kingship.

Shah Jahan ruled India with his queen Mumtaz Mahal by his side. She was his trusted advisor and was even given the power to make orders that had to be carried out by government officials. But she was also his close friend and his wife. The king brought her many gifts, including diamonds and roses, and had special rooms built for her in the palace.

In the third year of his rule, Shah Jahan went to war to win control of more areas of southern India. The queen went with him even though she was pregnant with their fourteenth child. While the king was conducting the war, Mumtaz Mahal had a healthy baby girl, but it was reported that she heard the baby cry before she was born. According to superstition, this was a bad sign.

The Emperor Shah Jahan

This drawing from Travels in the Mogul Empire, 1656–1668, *by Francois Bernier. (Westminster, England: Archibald Constable and Company, 1891)*

Soon, Shah Jahan was called to the bedside of his dying queen. According to legend, before the queen died, she whispered to Shah Jahan that she wanted him to build a monument so beautiful and perfect that people would be reminded of the power of love.

Construction of the Illumined Tomb

After Mumtaz Mahal died, the emperor was so overcome with grief that he locked himself in his rooms for eight days. When he finally came out, he seemed a lot older. According to a court historian, the emperor's beard, which had been black, turned more than one-third gray.

The same year that his queen died, Shah Jahan commanded that a monument to her must be started immediately. It would be called the Illumined Tomb by the Mogul people who built it.

No one is certain who the architect was, but the names of the builders who worked on different parts of the building and grounds were written down. The list shows how diverse a group they were. A Turk designed and built the domes. A man from Lahore, in what is now Pakistan, made the solid gold ornament

on top of the domes. Another Indian man was charged with making the mosaics.

The master calligrapher—the man who supervised the important art of hand lettering on the Taj Mahal—was from Persia. Many other Persian artists and businessmen came to manage the day-to-day activities of the massive building project.

From Baghdad, in what is now Iraq, and from Syria came two more calligraphers. From the present-day country of Kazakhstan came sculptors and a master stonecutter.

To this group of experts was added a workforce of 20,000 people. This small city became known as Mumtazabad, after the dead queen.

The main building material, marble, came from India, but other precious materials used to decorate the Taj Mahal had to come by caravan from far away. Jade and crystal came from China, chrysolite from Egypt, and turquoise from Tibet. Coral, mother-of-pearl, and rare shells came from the Indian Ocean.

Near the banks of the Jumna River the Taj Mahal slowly rose up. Shah Jahan was often there to see that the work was progressing as it should. Each year he held a memorial service for Mumtaz Mahal.

At last, when the tomb was finished, a coffin-shaped monument in memory of the queen was placed inside. Shah Jahan covered the coffin with pearls and a solid gold railing was built around it. (Later, the gold railing was replaced with a marble railing.) The best Persian carpets covered the interlocking designs of white marble and black stone in the floor. Candles in silver holders and gold lamps cast a soft glow; sweet-smelling incense filled the air.

Today, inside the Taj Mahal, you can still see the monument to Mumtaz Mahal. Beside it is another monument—the one for her husband, Shah Jahan, who died in 1666. The Persian carpets are gone, but incense still fills the air.

Think About It—

After reading this story, can you think of reasons why there would be no portraits of Mumtaz Mahal?

A Poem to Describe the Illumined Tomb

The Taj Mahal, in Agra, India, is a tomb built in the mid-1600's by a Muslim emperor in memory of his wife, who died in childbirth.

According to legend, Shah Jahan, the fifth Muslim ruler of India, promised his dying wife Mumtaz Mahal that he would build a monument to her memory and to the power of love.

Whether or not this is true, no one knows, but most people who see it agree that the Taj Mahal is one of the most beautiful buildings in the world. It is built of white and light-colored marble and decorated with designs and Arabic writing made of inlaid stones, such as turquoise and jade. Exquisitely carved stone flowers, vines, and other designs decorate the walls.

Perfectly laid out gardens and pools lead up to the entrance. Inside the tomb are the monuments to the queen and her devoted husband.

The muslim rulers called the Taj Mahal the Illumined Tomb. A poet named Kalim of Shah Jahan's court compared the Illumined Tomb to wonders of the sky. He said its color was like "dawn's bright face" and its beauty was as delicate as a cloud. He marvelled at the talents of the workers who almost brought stone to life with their exquisitely carved flowers and mosaics of carnelian and amber set in marble. He was sure that the beauty of the Illumined Tomb would impress the heart and soul of the emperor's beloved queen.

◆ *Objective:* To create a poem in celebration of a beautiful building or another man-made structure

◆ *Time to Complete Activity:* 1 hour

◆ *Materials Needed:* Paper, pencil, dictionary

Directions:

_____ Think of a building, bridge, or other man-made structure that you think is beautiful or interesting.

_____ Write a poem or description that expresses your thoughts and feelings about that building or struc-ture. To get started, try to remember your thoughts and feelings when you first saw the building. Jot down as many details as you can before you start writing.

Name _____

Date _____

Discovering the Underlying Grid of the Taj Mahal

The Taj Mahal, in Agra, India, is a tomb built in the mid-1600's by a Muslim emperor in memory of his wife, who died in childbirth.

According to legend, Shah Jahan, the fifth Muslim ruler of India, promised his dying wife Mumtaz Mahal that he would build a monument to her memory and to the power of love.

Whether or not this is true, no one knows, but most people who see it agree that the Taj Mahal is one of the most beautiful buildings in the world. It is built of white and light-colored marble and decorated with designs and Arabic writing made of inlaid stones, such as turquoise and carnelian. Exquisitely carved stone flowers, vines, and other designs decorate the walls. In the style that came from Persia, gardens, walkways, and pools that lead up to the entrance were designed in repeating patterns. They are also symmetrical—that is, the designs on one side of the central walkway repeat exactly on the other side. Inside the tomb are the monuments to the queen and her devoted husband. These monuments, the walls, floors, and ceilings also have repeating symmetrical designs.

The builders of the Taj Mahal used a grid (a pattern of horizontal and vertical lines forming squares of the same size) to design the building and its grounds.

- ◆ *Objective:* To discover the underlying grid of the Taj Mahal and grounds
- ◆ *Time to Complete Activity:* 1 hour
- ◆ *Materials Needed:* Pencil, this sheet, copy machine, ruler

---

Directions:

_____ If you wish, enlarge the drawing on this page.

_____ Using your pencil and ruler, draw the grid that you think the builders used to make sure that buildings, gardens, and walkways fit into a perfect pattern. (Several squares from the grid have already been drawn to get you started.)

(Adapted from Carroll et al., *The Taj Mahal*)

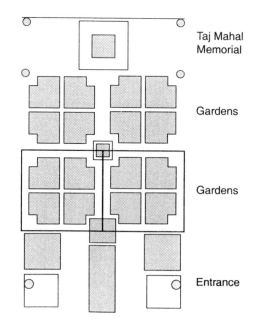

Taj Mahal
Memorial

Gardens

Gardens

Entrance

Name _____

Date _____

The Mosaics of the Taj Mahal

The Taj Mahal, in Agra, India, is a tomb built in the mid-1600's by a Muslim emperor in memory of his wife, who died in childbirth.

According to legend, Shah Jahan, the fifth Muslim ruler of India, promised his dying wife Mumtaz Mahal that he would build a monument to her memory and to the power of love.

Whether or not this is true, no one knows, but most people who see it agree that the Taj Mahal is one of the most beautiful buildings in the world. It is built of white and light-colored marble and decorated with designs and Arabic writing made of inlaid stones, such as turquoise and carnelian. This technique of setting small pieces of tile or stone in cement to make a design is called mosaic.

Inside the tomb are the monuments to the queen and her devoted husband. These monuments, the walls, floors, and ceilings also have mosaic designs made of marble and precious stones.

- ◆ *Objective:* To make a mosaic design
- ◆ *Time to Complete Activity:* 1–2 hours
- ◆ *Materials Needed:* Scraps or whole sheets of dark construction paper, white construction paper, scissors, copy machine, glue

---

Directions:

_____ Enlarge the design on this page to fit on an 8½ by 11 inch sheet of paper. (Enlarge the design as much as you want, but each piece needs to be enlarged the same amount.)

_____ Cut the design apart so you have individual petals and stems to use as patterns. The stems will have to be cut into sections.

_____ Place the flower and stem patterns on the dark construction paper, trace around them, and cut them out.

_____ Glue the flower and stem pieces to a sheet of white paper, re-forming the original design.

This is typical of designs that frame the arched doorways of the Taj Mahal. (Source: Dover Publications, Inc.)

Name _____

Date _____

Thought/Discussion Questions

1. Shah Jahan enjoyed watching prisoners being tortured and elephants fighting. On the other hand, he was a romantic who brought his wife gifts like roses and diamonds and created a magnificent tomb to her memory when she died. What do you think about these different sides of the emperor's personality? Have you read about other kings or queens who were cruel sometimes and nice at other times?

_____

_____

_____

_____

_____

2. The Persian-inspired designs that the architects and builders of the Taj Mahal used are very symmetrical—that is, patterns on one side of a center line repeat on the other side, and the two sides balance each other exactly. Can you think of a design on a building, a garden plan, or another man-made structure that is symmetrical? Do you like this kind of design or do you prefer a design that allows more natural lines?

_____

_____

_____

_____

_____